*Scottish Histories*

# KINGS AND QUEENS OF SCOTLAND

*Scottish Histories*

# KINGS AND QUEENS OF SCOTLAND

WAVERLEY
BOOKS

Published 2008 by Geddes & Grosset,
David Dale House, New Lanark, ML11 9DJ, Scotland

ISBN 9781 902407 66 1

Printed and bound in India

# CONTENTS

# CHAPTER I

# THE EDGE OF EMPIRE

Not until AD 80, when the Roman legions led by Julius Agricola first wound over the Cheviots into the country of the Caledonians, can the history of Scotland be said to begin. Of what happened before no record is left; no coin preserves the name of a king, no altar the name of a god. Our knowledge even of the succeeding century has been gained not so much from the pages of Tacitus and his fellow historians as from stones, pieces of armour and fragments of pottery, and at the end of that century darkness closes in once more.

Agricola found himself among unfamiliar peoples, red-haired and large-limbed, in a mountainous country where the hillsides were covered with woods and where marshes filled the hollows. No enemy attacked him, and he was able to build and garrison forts before he went into winter quarters.

In the following year he tightened his hold on the lands that he had overrun and in the summer of AD 83 began a campaign that was intended to destroy the Caledonian power once and for all. When he marched northward this time, his army kept in touch with the fleet, which hugged the coast and raided the harbours of the enemy.

But the advance of Agricola, although it at first stupefied the enemy, soon roused them to a fiercer resistance than they had previously shown. Fort after fort was attacked, and to this day the sixfold ditch at Ardoch, the rows of pits that defend Roughcastle, show how much the Roman legionary feared the mad rush of the Caledonian. Some of Agricola's officers advised a retreat, but, dividing his army into three parts, he pushed northwards.

He was soon to learn something of the spirit of the Caledonians. One night they surrounded the camp of the weakened Ninth Legion, slew the sentinels and, bursting through the gates, rushed on their sleeping enemies. The Romans were all but overwhelmed, when a shout was heard outside, and through the dim light of dawn they discerned the standards of Agricola's division. The Caledonians hesitated; the Romans within the camp, anxious to avoid the shame of needing reinforcements, fell on them furiously and drove them back through the gates. The Romans now seemed to have an opportunity of inflicting a crushing blow on the enemy, but the Caledonians soon vanished among the woods and marshes. A disaster had been barely averted; nothing substantial had been gained.

Agricola now advanced far into Perthshire and encamped for the winter at Inchtuthill, near the junction of the Tay and the Earn. Not until late in the summer of AD 84 did he resume his march against the still unsubdued Caledonians. As before, his fleet crept along the coast, plundering and burning, while he, at the head of a flying column, plunged into the northern forests and came upon 30,000 Caledonians posted on the slopes of Mons Graupius under the leadership of Calgacus.

The battle was hard fought. The Caledonians, although they charged wildly, found that their small shields and long, unpointed swords could work little harm on the great shields of the Roman troops who stabbed with their short, keen

8

swords. The ranks of the Caledonians broke and they were forced slowly up the hill. Meantime the Roman cavalry had routed the chariots and, galloping uphill, plunged into the struggling mass. Eventually the ranks of the Caledonians grew thin. Some fled, some held their ground, and some, although their weapons were lost, flung themselves upon the Romans in a last desperate charge. But the end could not be long delayed. Soon the ground was clear except for weapons and bodies of the slain, and the Caledonians were fleeing to the woods with the Romans in pursuit. The victory was not yet assured, for when the Caledonians reached the woods they rallied and fell hotly upon the foremost Romans. But at Agricola's command the cavalry were told to move forward in unbroken order and sweep the woods like a dragnet. At the sight of the long glittering lines advancing through the forest the Caledonians fled and did not rally again.

All that night above the din of the revelling soldiers could be heard the wailing of men and women. The Caledonians were wandering over the battlefield, dragging off their wounded. Next day no sound came from the woods, on the hills there was no gleam of weapons. Here and there a cloud of smoke rolled up to the sky. The Caledonians had fired their houses and withdrawn where Agricola could not pursue.

As the summer was far spent, Agricola had to remain content with this barren victory and retired slowly southwards to his winter quarters. Meantime the fleet, which had been ordered to proceed on a voyage of discovery, steered for the north. A landing was made on Orkney. Far on the northern horizon the sailors saw Shetland, which they took to be the islands of Thule, at that time believed to be the most northerly inhabited region of the world. From Orkney they sailed down the western coast, picking their way through sounds

**9**

and long sea lochs until they came to a part of the coast that they recognized and were able to assure themselves of what had long been guessed, that Britain was an island.

In the following year Agricola was recalled – because of the jealousy of the Emperor Domitian, Tacitus says; more probably because the Caledonian forests were swallowing up troops needed to meet the pressure of the barbarians on the Danube and the Rhine. The northern forts were abandoned, although in the south Newstead remained occupied for several years. In the bitter words of the historian, 'Britain had been conquered and at once thrown away.'

Of what happened in Scotland during the next fifty years no historian has left a record. We can imagine the Caledonian hordes sweeping across the isthmus into the south and throwing themselves on the forts that marked the Roman frontier. The battered helmet masks, cloven skulls and broken swords that have been dug up from Newstead tell a tale of desperate fighting, ending in the capture or evacuation of the fort.

So indomitable seemed these Caledonians, or so worthless their country, that when Hadrian fixed the boundary of the Roman province about the year 122 he chose neither the isthmus of the Forth and Clyde nor the northern side of the Cheviots, but the space between the Solway and the Tyne. But even Hadrian's wall of turf, defended by forts, could not overawe northern Britain, and about 140 the governor Lollius Urbicus advanced into Scotland with the Second, Sixth and Twentieth Legions, defeated the Caledonians and occupied the isthmus between Forth and Clyde.

Probably incursions from the north accounted for this forward movement. At any rate, Lollius Urbicus determined to lessen the danger of invasion by a permanent occupation of southern Scotland. The road from Corbridge to the shores of the Forth was again opened up, and Newstead and the other deserted forts that once guarded it were reconstructed and garrisoned. A wall of turf, about thirty-six miles long, was built between the Clyde and the Forth. It was defended at intervals of about two miles by forts and still further strengthened by a ditch, forty feet broad, that extended in front of it. Behind the rampart, joining fort to fort, stretched the military way along which troops could be hurried when the beacons on the signal mound spread news of invasion. About the year 143 the wall was completed. The legions withdrew to their bases in southern Britain and were replaced by auxiliaries, Gauls, Germans, Thracians and Syrians.

The occupation of Scotland was now as complete as it was ever to be. It was never more than a military occupation. We do not find, as in southern Britain, towns planned after the Roman fashion with forum and basilica, inhabited by Britons who used Latin as their ordinary speech. Each community lived its own life, in the midst of a hostile population that was ready to break into rebellion at a moment's notice.

As to the purpose of the wall, one must remember that it was not meant to be an impregnable barrier, a huge fortress thirty-six miles long defending southern Britain, as the lines of Torres Vedras defended Lisbon in the Napoleonic Wars. Its garrison of ten thousand could not possibly hold such an extended line against the combined forces of the Caledonians. It was designed not to suppress rebellion but to prevent rebellion breaking out. At the least sign of disturbance on the northern side of the wall beacons would be lit and detachments hurried along from the nearest forts so that the disturbers of the peace might be crushed at once.

How helpless the garrisons were in the face of a general rising was shown in the year 155. In that year the Brigantes,

whose territory stretched from the Peak District to the Cheviots, rose in rebellion and hurled themselves upon the Roman forts. The northern wall was abandoned, again Newstead was captured, and although reinforcements were hurried from Germany, at least three years passed before the forts
could be won back and the ruined buildings restored. The
peace was only temporary. In 162 there was another rising, in
which some of the frontier forts were lost for a time.

Everyone knew that the end was not far off. The new
buildings were constructed carelessly, as if by men who had
lost heart or knew that their stay would be short. In another
twenty years the end came. As Commodus was ascending the
throne, the north again flamed out into rebellion, and in 184
he took the title of Britannicus as a sign that the rebellion had
been subdued. It was an empty boast. Hadrian's Wall had indeed been won back from the rebels, but, except for one or
two outlying posts, all north of it was abandoned. Somewhere about 183 the final evacuation took place. The distance slabs in the great wall, which the legionaries had fixed
proudly forty years before, were buried face downwards, the
altars were thrown into pits or wells, the stone buildings par-
tially demolished and the wooden barracks set on fire. We can
see the long line of the cohorts tramping along the southern
road, their Roman officers looking sullenly back to where
the smoke of the abandoned forts hung low on the horizon.
Newstead and Birrens, the chief strongholds in southern
Scotland, were also evacuated, their altars buried, their wells
choked with stones and rubbish, and with this the Roman
occupation of Scotland came to an end.

Yet this was not the last time that Roman troops were to be
seen on the soil of Scotland. In the year 208 the aged Emperor Septimius Severus entered Scotland to chastise the Cal-

12

edonians and the Maeatae, as the inhabitants of the northern and southern parts beyond the wall were now called. He found himself in a country of barren mountains and marshy plains, fighting with an enemy that would not risk a pitched battle. Strange stories have come down to us of roads cut through forests, of morasses filled, of rivers bridged, of men swept away by floods, or ambushed by the enemy, or dispatched by their comrades when they lagged behind, till fifty thousand lives had been lost. Of what actually happened we can say little, although the spade of the archaeologist may some day furnish a solution to the mystery. It matters little; even if Severus did penetrate to the extremity of the island, even if he did force a peace from the Caledonians, before he died in 211 both Maeatae and Caledonians had risen in rebellion, and he knew that the work of conquest would have to be done again. It was never attempted. His son withdrew from the struggle, and Hadrian's Wall, which he had reconstructed, became for two centuries the limit of the Roman province. During these two centuries, although the tribes north of the wall had much to do with the fortunes of Roman Britain, no Roman soldier, so far as we know, set foot in the regions beyond the Cheviots.

Thus a hundred and thirty years separates the first and last Roman invasion of Scotland. The actual occupation lasted only forty years, and once during that period the Romans had to loose their hold of all the territory north of the Cheviots. In short, the history of the Romans in Scotland is one of fierce, profitless frontier fighting, leading at the best to a precarious military occupation. Nothing was gained, not even safety, by the occupation of the northern frontier, and the Caledonians in turn gained nothing from Roman civilization.

What manner of men were these barbarians who twice within thirty years drove the Romans from the Antonine Wall? Before the dawn of history, Scotland, and indeed the whole of Britain, had been peopled by a race with dark hair and long skulls, makers of tools of polished stone. But it was not by this race that Caesar and Agricola were confronted. Some centuries before the Romans set foot in Britain, a horde of strangers with broad skulls and fair hair had crossed from the continental Europe and settled in the island. They were Celts, the ancestors of the Scottish Highlanders of the present day. This first wave of invasion was followed by a second, that of the Brythons, another Celtic people, speaking a slightly different language, before whom the first invaders were forced to retreat into the west and north. When Agricola invaded Scotland, the Brythons had occupied all the south of the country except Galloway and the southern shore of the Firth of Forth, and a Brythonic tribe had even pushed to the north of the Forth.

What became of the aborigines is uncertain. Probably many battles took place in which the stone axe rattled against the bronze shield of the Celtic warrior, until the older race was either exterminated or forced to adopt the language and habits of the conquerors. With the possible exception of one or two place names, not a word of their tongue has survived.

For a description of the customs and appearance of these early inhabitants of Scotland one has little material but vague travellers' tales. In his account of the remoter parts of the island, Caesar tells us that the inhabitants were ignorant of weaving, clothing themselves only in skins, and that groups of ten or twelve men held their wives in common. As he did not himself penetrate more than thirty miles north of the Thames, however, he is probably repeating a description

**14**

given by the more civilized Britons of the south. His account of the marriage customs of these northerly peoples gains support from the fact that in the later Pictish kingdom succession was through the female. Tacitus, on the other hand, describes Calgacus as encouraging the Caledonians to fight by reminding them of their wives and homes. Of their appearance and methods of fighting he tells us that they had ruddy locks and were large of limb. They fought on foot, with small shields and long, unpointed swords, but some tribes used war chariots. The veteran soldiers wore trophies of their former battles. Their national organization seems to have been loose. The army that fought at Mons Graupius consisted of warriors from many tribes, owing allegiance to no supreme head, for even Calgacus is not described as a king – he is simply 'one excelling the other generals in bravery and rank'. Other evidences we can get from archaeology – the presence in the crannogs of red Samian ware from the workshops of Gaul shows that these strange lake dwellings were in use at this period. They were to be found in many a Scottish loch – natural or artificial islands, covered with a wooden platform, on which were erected large tent-like wooden huts. That these peoples were far from unskilled in metalwork the swords of bronze and the slender golden torch found at Newstead bear ample witness.

# CHAPTER II

# *T*HE COMING OF THE SCOTS

For about eighty years after the death of Severus, Roman Britain remained at peace. The great barrier of Hadrian, with its outlying fortresses, effectually kept back the barbarians of the north and allowed Roman customs and the Latin language to be adopted by the southern Briton. The first rumour of coming trouble was heard about the year 286, when Carausius, the commander of the *classis Britannica*, the Roman army in Britain, claimed to be the equal of the Emperors Diocletian and Maximian. His demand was unwillingly granted, but in 293 he was murdered by Allectus, one of his officers. Three years later Emperor Constantius Chlorus invaded Britain, and Allectus was defeated and slain. About the same time Germanic pirates began to harass the southern and eastern coasts of Britain. About half a century later, the Picti, or Picts, as the Romans called the painted barbarians of Scotland, began to make raids into the north of the province, while the west was exposed to the inroads of the Scoti, the Goidelic Celts of Ireland.

This is the first appearance of the Scots in history. At this time there was not a single Scot north of the Cheviots, and it must be remembered that it was not until the tenth century, five hundred years after the Scots had settled in it, that the country began to get the name of Scotland.

About the year 343 the Emperor Constans crossed to Britain and drove back the raiders, but the effect of his campaign was only temporary. Seventeen years later a more terrible invasion began. Saxons, Scots, Picts and Atacotts (probably the natives of Galloway) burst into the province, drove back the troops that had marched to meet them, stormed the great fortresses and penetrated far into the south of the island. The invaders seem to have intended to settle in the land that they had conquered, and although a general was sent from Gaul, he could do little. For eight years this state of turmoil continued, until in 368 Theodosius, the ablest general in the Roman Empire, had to be dispatched to Britain. Landing with a large army, he drove the invaders from the south of the island, then in the following year he marched north, clearing out the barbarians and restoring the towns and fortresses that had been destroyed. Once again Hadrian's Wall was the boundary of the province.

But the great Roman Empire was beginning to fall to pieces. The story of revolt and invasion was repeated in all its provinces, and every provincial general could now aspire to the imperial purple. In 383 Magnus Maximus, a Spanish officer in the British army, proclaimed himself emperor and, after driving back the marauding Picts and Scots, crossed to Gaul with a large army. He conquered western Europe and entered Italy itself, but in 388 he was defeated and slain by the legitimate emperors. Again Picts, Scots and Saxons poured into the weakened province, until, in the closing years of the fourth century, Stilicho, the minister of the Emperor Honorius, dispatched troops to Britain 'who bridled the Saxon and the Scot'. But the respite was brief. Rome itself was threatened, and in 402 the reinforcements sent by Stilicho were withdrawn for the defence of Italy. On the last

**17**

night of 406 the great raid on Rome took place, and in 410 Honorius wrote to the cities of Britain urging them to look to their own safety. Britain was no longer part of the Empire.

To the Briton of the south, whose mother tongue was Latin, whose house, with its tessellated floors and painted walls, aped the fashions of Italy, who loitered in baths and gaming houses, and did not worship the spirits of earth and water, as his fathers had done, but sacrificed to Jupiter or stood with outstretched hands in a Christian church, this must have seemed the end of all things. The work of three and a half centuries was undone. The arts and graces of civilization counted for nothing. He would prevail against the barbarian who had most of the barbarian in his nature.

But before the Romans had departed from Britain an event of the greatest importance took place in the country of the Picts. Until the early twentieth century, at the entrance to the deserted burying ground of Kirkmadrine in Wigtownshire, were sited two narrow, flat slabs, about five feet high, bearing upon them the cross of Constantine surrounded by a circle. Inscribed on one are the mystic letters A et Q, and the following words, cut in bold Roman characters: *Hic iacent s[an]c[t]i et praecipui sacerdotes Ides[us] Viventius et Maiorius* ('Here lie the sacred and outstanding priests Viventius and Maiorius'). These stones are probably relics of the mission of St Ninian, the first Christian teacher who penetrated north of the Solway.

Ninian was born in Britain about the middle of the fourth century. His father was a Christian and a man of rank. While he was a youth, when the connection between Britain and the rest of the Empire was still unbroken, he made his way to Rome, where he lived for many years. At length he was consecrated bishop, and he set out on his journey homewards along the great road that stretched through Gaul. He halted at Tours so that he might meet St Martin, and from him procured masons to build a church of stone. So in time Candida Casa, 'the Church of White Stone', rose at Whithorn on the northern shore of the Solway, but before it was completed, in the autumn of 397, news came that St Martin of Tours was dead, whereupon Ninian resolved that the church should be dedicated to him. For some years Ninian preached to the Galwegians and southern Picts, and made converts, but if he had hoped that his teaching would quell the savagery of the Picts and make them less eager for the plunder of southern Britain, he was cruelly disappointed.

After Ninian's death many of his converts lapsed into paganism. It was not until missionaries came from Ireland that Christianity became the abiding belief of the natives of Scotland. At this period Ireland was a heathen country, but about 432 St Patrick, a Briton, crossed the western seas, and in a comparatively short time the greater part of the island came under the influence of the Christian faith.

Meanwhile the plight of southern Britain was growing steadily worse. By the middle of the fifth century the Germanic sea rovers had gained a firm footing on the eastern and southern coasts, and a grim secular struggle began between them and the Britons. Soon they had swarmed over the central plains, stamping out the memorials of a civilization they did not understand, until they came to the western uplands. There they had to deal with a hardier folk, and there for a time the tide of conquest was arrested.

Once more the Scots appeared on the scene. They were Goidelic Celts who dwelt in the northeast corner of Ireland, in a district called Dalriada, and spoke a language that resembled that of the Picts more than that of the Britons. They had probably come under the influence of St Patrick and received the semblance, at least, of Christianity. In 498 Fergus Mor with a band of these Dalriada Scots crossed from Ireland and settled in what is now the county of Argyll. For about sixty years they not only held their own against the Picts whom they had displaced but added to their territories, until in 560 they were attacked by Brude, the Pictish king, and defeated in a battle in which their king, Gabran, was slain.

About thirteen years previously another people had made a settlement in the southeast of Scotland. In 547 Ida, a king of the Angles, had seized and fortified Bamburgh and made it the centre of his kingdom of Bernicia, which extended from the Tees to the Forth.

In the year 560, then, the country that we now call Scotland was divided among four or five different races. The district between the Firth of Forth and the Tweed formed the northern part of the kingdom of Bernicia, occupied by the Angles, a Teutonic race speaking a language quite different from that of the neighbouring peoples. The southwestern part, with the exception of the district west of the River Nith, formed part of the still unconquered territory of the Britons, which at this time in the western area extended without a break as far as Cornwall. The district west of the Nith was occupied by a Pictish people. In the west Dalriada, consisting of the peninsula of Kintyre, belonged to the Scots, who at this period were ruled by King Conall, while to the east and north of Dalriada stretched the wide territories of the Picts.

Although the Picts of the south had been influenced by the teaching of Ninian, the northern Picts were still heathen. No knowledge of their gods has come down to us. They seem to have worshipped the forces of nature, the spirits of the winds and the waters. We read, for instance, that they worshipped a fountain that was the haunt of demons and had magical properties. They held in great reverence the druids, or magicians, men who claimed power to control the elements and call up storms at will. On sculptured stones found in what was once the territory of the Picts we see strange figures recurring again and again – a crescent intersected by two decorated rods, and a double circle crossed by a zigzag line. These occur sometimes alone, sometimes along with a cross. Symbols they must be, but what they mean no one can tell. They were probably pagan symbols that in the course of time were adopted by the Christian monks and invested with a new significance, just as that haunted fountain was worshipped by the Pictish converts after it had been blessed by Columba.

After Patrick's mission to Ireland, Christianity spread rapidly and a great church soon arose, a church throbbing with life and aflame with enthusiasm. This enthusiasm sometimes overflowed in a fantastic asceticism or in the unwearying labours of the illuminator, bending for days over one page of the sacred book. It took a far nobler form in the missionary zeal that drove its monks not only into Scotland and England but into countries as far distant as Gaul and Switzerland.

The church was purely monastic, divided into communities, each settled on its allotted portion of the land of the tribe, each ruled over by its abbot. Its doctrines at this time were the same as those of the church on continental Europe, although there were differences in some external details. Although a priest could be ordained only by a bishop, and although when a bishop was present no priest could celebrate the Eucharist, in all other cases the bishop was under the jurisdiction of the abbot of his monastery, who was often simply in priest's orders. In the method of fixing the date of

Easter and in the fashion of the priest's tonsure it differed from the Roman church – a circumstance that a century afterwards resulted in bitter strife.

In this church St Columba, or Columcille, was reared, and in it he rose to eminence, founding many churches and monasteries. In 561 Columba, enraged by what he considered the injustice of King Diarmaid, stirred up the men of Connaught and the north to attack him. The result was the battle of Cul-Drehme, in which Diarmaid was routed. But the conduct of Columba in provoking strife was censured. A synod met to excommunicate him, and he was saved only by the intercession of St Brendan. According to legend, he went to his confessor and was absolved on condition that he left Ireland forever and saved as many souls as there had been men lost in the battle. This story is almost certainly mythical, but remorse had probably some part in inducing him to seek the western islands of Scotland. Other things must have persuaded him – the perilous straits to which the little kingdom of Dalriada had been reduced by the heathen Picts, and the missionary zeal that burned with unabated fire throughout his life.

In the year 563, with twelve followers, Columba set sail for Scotland. He was kindly received by King Conall, who granted the island of Iona to him and his monks. Iona is a small island off the coast of Mull, about three miles long and a mile and a half broad. It is rugged, but with no hills of considerable height except Dun-I, in the northern part, which rises to about 600 feet. Here, between the foot of the hill and the eastern shore of the island, Columba fixed the site of his monastery.

Two years later he made his way to the palace of the Pictish king, near the banks of the River Ness. When he and his companions arrived they found the gates of the enclosure barred against them, whereupon, it is said, Columba made the sign of the cross on the gates and knocked, at which they immediately flew open. The king, impressed by the miracle, advanced to meet Columba, received him respectfully and ever after held him in high esteem. It is certain that within a short time King Brude became a convert to Christianity and that many of his people followed his example and embraced the new faith. We can imagine the aged druids listening sullenly to the new doctrine or flushing with anger when their magical powers were attributed to the help of evil spirits. To doubt the pretensions of these magicians never entered into the heads of Columba and his followers. They believed in demons as they did in angels, in the efficacy of a charm as well as of a blessing. If a contrary wind arose, it was the work of the druids; if it fell suddenly, a miracle had been worked by their prayers. It was only natural that the druids should try to hinder Columba in his work, but when they tried to interrupt him as he was chanting the evening psalms he sang in a voice 'like pealing thunder', and when they persuaded him to drink from an enchanted fountain, the waters of which dealt disease to all who tasted them, he drank and was unhurt.

So Columba returned to Iona, joyful because, after venturing with a small band of monks over mountain passes and lochs and desolate moorlands into the heart of a hostile country, he had planted the seeds of his faith among the nation of the Picts and gained the friendship of a king whose authority was recognized from Orkney to the Firth of Forth. But he was not satisfied. Again and again he returned to the kingdom of the Picts, burning with eagerness to carry his message to places where it had not yet been heard. Monasteries were founded in many of the western islands as well as on the mainland, and Christianity was firmly established.

**23**

But Columba was not only a great missionary, the founder and organizer of a great church; his opinion in state affairs counted for much. In 574 King Conall died, and Columba persuaded the Scots to choose the energetic Aiden as his successor in place of Eoganan, his elder brother. In the following year, along with King Aiden, Columba attended the Synod of Drumceatt, in Ireland, where the Scots of Dalriada were freed from the tribute they had been compelled to pay to the Irish king, although they had still to join him in his warlike expeditions.

In 584 Brude, the king of the Picts, died and was succeeded by Gartnaidh, whose royal seat seems to have been in the southern part of the Pictish kingdom. The foundation of churches at Abernethy and St Andrews shows that Christianity was penetrating to parts of the country where its preachers had never been heard before or had been heard only to be forgotten.

But the spread of Christianity did not put an end to the struggle between the different races of Scotland, as is shown in a strange story told by Adamnan. 'At another time . . . he suddenly said to his servant Diormit: "Ring the bell." The brethren, roused by the sound, ran quickly to the church, with the holy prelate himself at their head. There he began, on bended knees, to say to them: "Let us pray now earnestly to the Lord for this people and King Aiden, for at this hour they are engaged in battle." Then after a short time he went out of the oratory, and looking up to heaven said: "Now the barbarians are fleeing and to Aiden the victory has been given, a sad one though it be."'

This was the battle of Chirchind, fought against the Miathi, probably a Pictish tribe, in which the eldest sons of the king were slain.

# CHAPTER III

# TWO CENTURIES OF STRIFE

Columba died in 597 and the history of Scotland for the two and a half centuries that followed his death is a barren record of battles and the deaths of kings. Sometimes the Scots of Dalriada were fighting with the Britons of Strathclyde, sometimes Scot and Pict, led by kings of whom no memory survives except an empty name, clashed together on forgotten fields, sometimes the Angles of Northumbria warred against Pict or Briton. Now the chiefs of rival tribes were battling for the throne of Dalriada. At another time four claimants to the Pictish crown were fighting with one another. Even the church was not free from strife: the followers of Columba refused to sit at table with the Roman priests. But in all this confusion, among these dim, ever moving figures of warring kings and angry ecclesiastics, these glimpses of wounded men and burning churches, of pirate hulks sweeping the western seas, we can distinguish the beginnings of national unity. Before the two centuries and a half are ended Scots and Picts have been brought together under one king.

At the time of Columba's death the king of Bernicia was Ethelfrith, an ambitious monarch who made war on the Britons and added much of their territory to his domains. In 603 Aiden, the king of Dalriada, jealous of his growing power, marched against him, and a fierce battle took place at

Degsastan, which ended in the utter defeat of the Scots. 'Never from that time,' says the English monk and historian, the Venerable Bede, 'has any of the kings of Scots even to this day dared to come to battle in Britain against the nation of the Angles.' But Ethelfrith's ambition was not satisfied. In 606 he drove Edwin, the ruler of Deira, from his kingdom, and for eleven years ruled over a realm stretching from the Humber to beyond the Tweed, until in 617 Edwin returned from exile and defeated the usurper. The sons of Ethelfrith and many of the young nobles escaped to the country of the Scots, where they were instructed in the Christian faith and baptised. In 633 the British king Cadwallon and Penda, the heathen king of Mercia, joined forces and attacked Edwin, whom they slew at Hatfield. For a year Enfrith, the eldest son of Ethelfrith, reigned over Bernicia, but he was slain, and in 634 his brother Oswald came to the throne.

This event gave Celtic Christianity another opportunity of showing its missionary zeal, the zeal that forty years before had sent Columbanus and his monks as far as Gaul and Switzerland. At King Oswald's request a bishop was sent into his realm from the Scottish church. But the Angles were unmoved by the new teaching, and the bishop returned to Iona, where in a council of the elders he denounced the people of Bernicia as intractable, hard and barbarous. In the discussion that followed, a monk named Aidan turned to the disappointed missionary and said: 'Meseemeth, brother, that thou hast been harder than was just for unlearned hearers, and hast not offered them, according to apostolic precept, first the milk of milder doctrine.' At these words all eyes were fixed on the speaker. His counsels of moderation gained the approval of the assembly, and it was agreed that he should be sent to the court of King Oswald.

The wisdom of this choice was soon apparent. The missionary shrank from no exertion, no privation that would bring him nearer the fulfilment of his purpose. He travelled all over Northumbria on foot, turning aside whenever he saw a chance of making a convert, exhorting rich and poor alike, never hesitating to rebuke a wrongdoer, however powerful. For wealth or the favour of the great he cared little. Money that was given to him he straightaway bestowed on the poor or used for the ransom of slaves. Much as he loved King Oswald, he would not tarry long at the royal banquet; when the king presented him with a horse it was at once given away as alms. Intolerant of idleness in himself, he would not allow it in his disciples but made them spend their leisure in reading or in learning psalms by heart.

At Lindisfarne, at Bamburgh, at many another place between the Humber and the Forth rose the little wooden churches with their thatched roofs, surrounded by the huts of the brethren, for in the Northumbrian church, as in the Celtic churches of Scotland and Ireland, all the clerics were monks.

Penda, however, again rallied the forces of heathenism, and in 642 Oswald was slain. He was succeeded by Oswin, but in 651 Oswin was killed by treachery, and 'the twelfth day after the slaying of the king whom he loved' Aidan died under the walls of his church at Bamburgh. Another bishop, Finan, was sent from Scotland, and Oswy ascended the throne of Northumbria. But the indomitable Penda made yet another attempt to overthrow the power of the Northumbrian king. Four years later heathen Mercians and half-heathen Britons gathered round him and followed him in his northward march against Oswy. Oswy's entreaties for peace, his promise of priceless gifts from the royal treasury, failed to move the fierce old heathen from his purpose, and he insisted upon

**27**

immediate battle. Somewhere in Lothian the struggle took place, but victory went to those who had looked for defeat and Penda was slain. From that day Oswy's power increased. As a result of his victory, the Mercians and Britons came under his sway. In 657 the death of his nephew Talorcen, king of the Picts, made the southern part of that nation subject to him, while the Scots of Dalriada seem to have owned him as their lord.

Meantime the power of the church was increasing in Northumbria. A few years before, a youth named Cuthbert had galloped up to the monastery of Melrose and, leaping from his horse, had asked to be received into the community. In due time he became prior of Melrose and among the zealous Scottish ecclesiastics distinguished himself by his ceaseless exertions.

Many of the wild Northumbrians were Christians only when they were well; when they fell ill they prayed to the old gods. Many, dwelling in remote villages among the mountains, had never heard the teaching of the monks. To these people especially Cuthbert addressed himself. The shepherd who had used a charm when he was ill did not dare to meet Cuthbert's piercing eyes but stammered out his fault. The men of remoter regions, whom previous missionaries had either despised or feared, listened eagerly to his simple, persuasive speech. Over many a trackless moorland, up many a lonely glen, did Cuthbert make his way, forgetful of hunger and fatigue, of the difficulties of the road and of the fierce disposition of the people. Such was his enthusiasm that he was absent from his monastery sometimes for weeks at a time.

But the church was now nearing a crisis in its history. In one or two of their customs the Columban clerics differed from the monks of the Roman church who had evangelized the south of England. The fashion of the tonsure differed, the Columban monks leaving the back of the head quite unshaven, and because the Columban church adhered to an older mode of calculating the date of Easter there was sometimes an interval of a few weeks between the celebrations of the festival. The first murmurs of the dispute had been heard in the time of Aidan, but the most bitter opponents of his doctrine were constrained to respect him for his goodness, and it was not till 664, three years after Aidan's successor had died and had been succeeded as Bishop of Lindisfarne by the Scottish bishop Colman, that the dispute finally came to a head.

The most vehement champion of the Roman way was Wilfred, Abbot of Ripon. The king, Oswy, who had spent his youth among the Scots, supported the Columban church but found his queen and his son Aldfrith ranged against him. To settle the matter the king commanded that a synod should be held in the abbey of Whitby and that the question should be debated in his presence by the Columban and Roman priests.

To Bishop Colman's arguments from antiquity and from the practice of St Columba Wilfred opposed the authority of St Peter. Even if Columba was a holy man and powerful in miracles, Wilfred urged, his example could not have more weight than that of St Peter, to whom had been entrusted the keys of heaven.

Here the king interrupted eagerly: 'Is it true, Colman, that these words were spoken to Peter by our Lord?'

'It is true, Oh King,' said Colman.

'Can you show any such power given to Columba?' was the next question. Colman had to answer: 'None.'

The king was not yet satisfied. 'Do you both agree,' he asked, 'that these words were principally directed to Peter and that the keys of heaven were given to him by our Lord?'

They answered: 'We do.'

Then the king said: 'And I also say unto you that he is the doorkeeper, whom I will not contradict, but will, as far as I know and am able, in all things obey his decrees, lest, when I come to the gates of the kingdom of heaven, there should be none to open them.'

The king's speech decided the matter. Reluctantly Colman had to leave his church at Lindisfarne and return to Iona, carrying with him part of the bones of Aidan. But although the Celtic church had fallen in England, it had fallen with honour, as the noble tribute of Bede, who 'detested much' its heresies, bears witness: 'Of how great frugality and of what continence were Colman and his predecessors, even the place which they ruled bore testimony. For when they departed very few houses were found there, excepting the church; that is, those only without which social intercourse could not exist at all. Apart from flocks they had no moneys. For if they had received any money from the rich, they gave it straightaway to the poor. For it was not necessary either that moneys should be gathered or that houses should be provided for the entertainment of the powerful of the world, since they never came to church except only for the sake of prayer or of hearing God's Word. The King himself, when occasion required, came with only five or six attendants; and departed when his prayer in the church was ended . . . . For the whole anxiety of these teachers was to serve God, not the world.'

The death of Oswy in 671, seven years after the Synod of Whitby, was the sign for the Picts to attempt to throw off the Northumbrian yoke. In the following year a great army of them marched southwards, but they were met by a force of cavalry under the youthful King Egfrith and sustained so crushing a defeat that, according to an old chronicler, two rivers were blocked with corpses. But their chance came thirteen years later, when Egfrith, disdaining the advice of Cuthbert, advanced into the territory of Brude, king of the Picts. The Picts retired before the invader and lured Egfrith north of the Firth of Tay. Then, when he had reached the swamp of Nechtansmere, beyond the Sidlaw Hills, they fell upon his army and cut it to pieces. The king himself was slain, and only a few of his followers escaped to tell the dreadful news.

With this battle ended the domination of Northumbria over the Picts and over the Britons of Strathclyde. Nor could the bishops of Lindisfarne any longer claim jurisdiction over the churches of Scotland.

But the dispute about Easter had not been ended by the Synod of Whitby. A difference of opinion on this question was beginning to show itself among the Celtic clergy of Scotland and Ireland who owed allegiance to Iona. The champion of the new order was none other than Adamnan, the pious and learned biographer of Columba, who after the death of Egfrith had visited Northumbria and had there been convinced of the justice of the Roman observance. But although many of the Irish monasteries that were under the rule of the abbot of Iona conformed to the new order, he could by no means persuade the Scottish monks, even those who lived in Iona, to forsake their old customs, and he died in 704 with his purpose unfulfilled.

Adamnan, however, had left behind him an enduring monument. In his life of Columba, cumbered as it is with tales of the miraculous, he did what no other Scottish scholar was to do for many a century: he described the society in which he lived, its beliefs and customs, and the character of the people amid which it was placed. Of course these vivid

**31**

little sketches are the result of so many happy accidents. When Adamnan tells how the saint expelled a demon from a milk pail, he expects the reader to be impressed by his hero's supernatural powers. The reader smiles at the miracle but thankfully accepts the information that the monks kept cows, that Columba lived in a little hut between the cowshed and the other buildings of the monastery and that the Christian monks believed in the existence of demons who could conceal themselves in a milk pail. But this is not the only merit that the book possesses. Adamnan has succeeded in his purpose. Columba, 'the soldier of Christ', lives again in his pages, and the story of his last days especially cannot fail to move by its beauty and pathos.

The changes that Adamnan had sought to bring about were not to be long delayed. About six years after his death, Nechtan, the king of the Picts, sent a letter to Ceolfrith, the abbot of Jarrow, asking his advice about the tonsure and the observance of Easter, and requesting that architects should be sent to build a church of stone in the Roman fashion. The reply, of course, advised conformity to the customs of the rest of Christendom, and Nechtan altered the date of Easter, made all priests shave the crown and drove the monks of Iona, who upheld the old usage, out of his kingdom into the west of Scotland. Soon afterwards, however, the community of Iona and the dependent monasteries, moved by the exhortations of Egbert, an exiled English priest, adopted the coronal tonsure and followed the orthodox mode of observing Easter. The supremacy of Iona over the churches of the Picts had come to an end.

It would be tedious to follow the endless strife that went on between the claimants to the throne of Dalriada or of the Pictish kingdom. It is little wonder that more than one king, tired of ruling a turbulent people, sought refuge in a monastery. It is little wonder that the monastery could not hold for long men who had spent all their days in fighting. In 723, for instance, Sealbach of Dalriada, who had deposed and slain his brother, retired to a monastery and was succeeded by his son Dungal. In the following year Nechtan, king of the Picts, copied his example and left the throne to King Drust. But in 726 the crown of Dalriada was seized by Eochaid, while the usurper's brother Alpin drove Drust from his throne. Sealbach left the quiet of the monastery and once more led his men to battle, but he was defeated.

Meantime the kingdom of the Picts was in an extraordinary plight. Alpin had to contend with a second usurper, Aengus, who met him in battle and defeated him. Later in the same year, Alpin met defeat at the hands of Nechtan, who, like Sealbach, had put off his robes of religion, but in the following year Aengus defeated first Nechtan and then Drust, and in 731 was firmly established on the Pictish throne.

This Aengus seems to have been a vigorous king. In 736 he ravaged Dalriada and captured Dunadd, its capital. Five years later he inflicted a crushing defeat on the Scots, and in 756, along with Eadbert of Northumbria, he led an army against Dumbarton, the chief town of Strathclyde, and forced the Britons to come to terms. It was in his reign that Bishop Acca fled from Hexham, bearing with him the relics of St Andrew, and on the promontory of Kilrymount, beside the humbler buildings dedicated to the Columban saint Regulus, a stone church was built and dedicated to St Andrew.

Although the Scots had received a crushing defeat at the hands of Aengus, they had not lost their independence. In 766 a battle took place between Kenneth, the Pictish king, and Aedh, king of Dalriada. But their power was fast dwin-

**33**

dling. In 781 Fergus, the successor of Aedh, died, and for sixty years after that Dalriada seems to have been governed directly by the Pictish kings.

And now, in the year 794, the galleys of the Danish pirates appeared in the western seas. In the following year Iona was plundered. Seven years later the monastery was burned, and in 806 the brethren were slaughtered by the Danes. Clearly an isolated, defenceless island like Iona was no place for a metropolitan church. The remains of Columba were carried to Ireland, and in 807 Abbot Cellach ordained that in future the monastery at Kells was to be regarded as the centre of the Columban order. But the zeal of earlier days had not departed from the church. A few years later the shrine of Columba was carried to Iona, and a church of stone was built to the south of the ancient wooden church, now a heap of ashes. To there in 825 came St Blathmac, 'coveting martyrdom'. Shortly after his arrival, news came to the monastery that pirates were at hand. Blathmac summoned the monks and told them of their danger. 'Whoever of you can face it,' he said, 'I pray you arm yourselves with courage, but those that are weak at heart and panic-stricken should hasten their flight.'

Some fled, a few remained. The bones of St Columba, enclosed in a curiously wrought shrine of gold and silver, were hidden in a place unknown to the abbot. Soon afterwards the clash of weapons and the wild shouts of the Danes were heard. They rushed into the church, slaying the monks and sparing only Blathmac in the hope that he would reveal where the shrine had been hidden. To their threats he gave the answer that he did not know where the shrine was. 'But if it were permitted me to know,' he added, 'never would these lips tell it to your ears. Savagely bring your swords, seize their hilts, and kill.' The dauntless Abbot gained what he had coveted. A few moments afterwards his body lay on the floor of the church, pierced by many swords.

But while the Danish pirates were sweeping the western seas or leaving heaps of smouldering ashes and murdered men to show where they had landed, a great revolution had taken place in the government of the country. In 839 King Eoganan led the Picts against the invaders and died in battle. This was an opportunity for the Scots, who for sixty years had been in subjection to the Pictish kings. Now that the Picts were crushed and their king slain, Kenneth, the son of Alpin, made himself king of the Scots, and in 844 he became king of the Picts also, ruling over practically the whole of Scotland north of the Firths of Forth and Clyde.

How all this happened is uncertain. According to an old story, the Scots invited the Pictish chiefs to a banquet, and, when the guests were dazed with wine, loosened the supports of their seats and slaughtered them as they rolled helpless on the ground. But this reads like the invention of an imaginative chronicler who had to explain how the chieftain of a small tribe was able to seize the throne of the powerful Pictish kingdom. It may be that Kenneth's father, Alpin, had married a Pictish princess and thus by the Pictish law of succession had given his son a claim to the crown. That is no more than a hypothesis; the exact truth will never be known.

# CHAPTER IV

# THE KINGDOM IS BORN

The king with whom the story of the kingdom of Scotland may be said to begin, therefore, is Kenneth, the son of Alpin. Scotland, in this dim remoteness of its history, has already encountered Christianity, but the country is still a division of kingdoms – four of them. There are the Picts in the north; there are the Scots (originally from what we know as Ireland) in Argyll; there are the Welsh Britons in Strathclyde; and there is Anglian Lothian, extension of the southern kingdom of Northumbria. With Kenneth, these four become three. He was king of the Scots of Argyll and appears to have reigned in Argyll for two years (841–43) before also becoming king of the Picts.

His sudden rise to power is surrounded with mystery. He lived in a time of great adventure and was a masterful and ambitious man, a farseeing statesman and capable military leader. The death of King Eoganan in battle was followed by confused conditions in the land of the Picts and afforded him an opportunity that he was not slow to take advantage of. He appears to have had, by reason of his royal Pictish descent, a claim to the throne, but it is uncertain whether or not he really established his power as a conqueror. There is little justification for the view that the Scots of Argyll subdued the Picts by force of arms after being themselves in a state of subjection for about a century. The revolution that occurred appears to have been mainly a political one.

Kenneth's real opponents were the Pictish princes of the royal line and the Pictish nobles, and there may be genuine historical fact in the persisting tradition that he got rid of them at a 'peace conference' that had been summoned to deal with the problem of succession to the throne. One of the lost tales of Ireland was entitled 'The Treachery of Scone', and the twelfth-century Welsh chronicler Giraldus Cambrensis may have heard a version of it, for he tells us that the Picts were superior to the Scots in arms and valour but were overcome by foul means. The Pictish nobles had been invited to a banquet, and their benches were fixed by bolts above pits that had been secretly dug. When the bolts were drawn out, the nobles dropped into the pits in which they were trapped up to the knees and were immediately assassinated.

We meet with a reference to this treachery in *Berchan's Prophecy*, which is extracted in Skene's *Picts and Scots*. It refers to Kenneth as *Ferbasach* (the 'conqueror' or 'slaughterer'), 'the first Irish king who will reign in the east, after using the strength of spears and of swords, after violent deaths, after violent slaughter. The fierce men in the east are deceived by him. They dig the earth (mighty is the art!), a deadly trap, death by wounding in the centre of Scone.'

In the *Chronicle of the Canons of Huntingdon*, a compilation of the thirteenth century, it is stated that Kenneth fought against the Picts 'seven times in one day'. This may be a reference to the murder of seven Pictish princes or nobles. The *Chronicle of Melrose*, however, credits Kenneth with 'many battles' and says he was the first to introduce 'Scottish laws' into the land of the Picts. The fourteenth-century Scottish chronicler John of Fordun may be sound in his view that the chief new law was that which regulated the succession to the throne, supplanting the Pictish law of inheritance by the female line.

Having got rid of the Pictish nobles, Kenneth appears to have supplanted them by men of his own. He must have had influential supporters among the Gaels who had already settled in the country and, no doubt, they welcomed his accession to the throne. He was also backed by the Columban party, for he was a champion of their church. In the seventh year of his reign, according to one chronicle, the relics of St Columba were conveyed to the church at Dunkeld, and the Columban clergy became once more a power in the land.

Kenneth mac Alpin was undoubtedly one of the great kings of ancient Scotland. Like Brude I, Brude III and Angus I, he was an outstanding champion of national independence and had a clear conception of the value of a strong centralized government. Although Ireland suffered greatly from Scandinavian raids and conquests, and England, weakened by internal rivalries, was doomed to fall like ripe fruit into Danish hands, the resistance of the united Picts was well maintained. There is only one record of a successful Danish raid. The pirates had come to know of the transference to Perthshire of the Columban relics and the jealously guarded treasure of the clergy, and they penetrated the country as far inland as Dunkeld. They do not appear, however, to have obtained what they sought. It was easier to conceal among the Highland mountains than in Iona the precious and sacred articles that attracted them, and it was less easy for them to retreat overland than overseas.

It is probable that this raid occurred when King Kenneth was absent on one of his military expeditions. He is said to have invaded Anglian territory six times and to have seized

**38**

and burned Dunbar and Melrose. Apparently he extended his rule over the eastern Lowlands, which had become semi-independent. According to the fourteenth-century compilation of Randolph Higden, he subdued Bernicia from the Forth to the Tweed. He seems also to have made conquests at the expense of the Strathclyde kingdom. The Britons of that area once raided the land of the Picts and burned Dunblane.

Kenneth is referred to by Duald MacFirbis as a man 'of many stables'. This significant statement indicates that he could mobilize a strong force of mounted men, and he may well have owed much of his success as a general to his mobile army. As we have seen, the Angles of Northumbria similarly made use of mounted forces in King Oswy's time. When the Pictish rising took place immediately after the death of Oswy, the Northumbrian general Beornheth won his victory between the two rivers in Manau with 'an army of cavalry'. The Danes in a similar manner made use of horses in war. When they undertook the conquest of England they landed on the coast and during the winter season scoured the country for horses. They then 'became', as Professor Collingwood has shown, 'a force of wonderfully active and mobile mounted infantry, like the hobelars of the thirteenth century or the Boers of recent times'.

Mobile on land and strong at sea, the Danes were more than a match for the Angles and Saxons. King Kenneth must have had his ships of war as well as 'many stables', for he set up a strong defence against Scandinavian aggression.

It would appear, too, that Kenneth was an able diplomat. His differences with the Britons were settled by an alliance that was confirmed by a royal marriage. One of his daughters married Run (pronounced *Roon*), the heir to the throne of Strathclyde. Another daughter, named Mael Muire, married

**39**

Aed Finnliath, king of Ireland, and their son, Niall Glun-dubh, became king of Ireland. Another daughter, named Muire, married the Irish prince Mael Mithigh, and their son, Conghalach, also became king of Ireland. According to Skene, a fourth daughter married Olaf the White, king of Dublin. This marriage, however, is very doubtful. There was more than one Olaf, and Olaf the White had, before he left Norway, married that famous lady Aud the Deep-minded, daughter of Ketil Flatnose and mother of Thorstein the Red. Another prominent Olaf was the son of Godfrey, a king of the Isles who had cooperated with King Kenneth before he became king of the Picts.

When King Kenneth died in 858, he was buried in Iona. His brother Donald, who succeeded him, is apparently the ruler referred to in *Berchan's Prophecy* as 'the son of a foreign woman'. We do not know, however, whether Donald's mother was Anglian, Danish or Norse. His father had evidently effected a diplomatic second marriage when his famous son Kenneth was having dealings with men like Godfrey.

King Donald reigned for only three years but in that time is said to have applied the laws of Dalriada to the Picts. He died at Scone, leaving the throne to Constantine, the son of Kenneth, who reigned for about fifteen years (862–77) as Constantine I although he was not the first king of that name in Scotland. With him begins a new phase of the Viking Age, for the period of raiding was being followed by a period of organized conquest and settlement.

# CHAPTER V

# WINTER WARRIORS IN THE VIKING AGE

'During the period of the Norse wars in Ireland,' writes Professor Eoin MacNeill, 'and for some centuries before and after it, the Irish had no permanent military organization. Their largest military operations never extended beyond a few weeks. Their fighting men were called out for the purpose from their ordinary peaceful occupations and could not lawfully be held to military service for more than a few weeks in any year. Thus there was no effective means of fighting down a hostile force encamped on its ships in a large inland water.'

The conditions in the land of the Picts, on the other hand, were different from those that obtained in Ireland. That part of Scotland was to a considerable extent one of stock-rearers and hunters. The coastal and island peoples had been seafarers from the earliest times of which we have knowledge, and apparently engaged in commerce as well as war. Like certain of the Norsemen, they went sometimes on trading voyages and sometimes on plundering expeditions. Customs that survived for several centuries in the crofting districts, especially in the west, indicate that women engaged to a large extent in agricultural operations, tilling the soil and reaping the harvest, while the men employed themselves at some distance from home. When cattle and sheep were driven to the summer grazings, they were looked after by young women who lived in those temporary habitations known nowadays as shielings. As in later times, the nobles mobilized each autumn large numbers of their tenants and retainers to engage in deer drives, bird shooting, and river fishing. Abundant supplies of salted flesh and fish were stored in fortresses and cottages for the winter season.

These hunting expeditions were conducted on a much larger scale in Scotland than in Ireland, and they continued for a long time to be an outstanding feature of Highland life. In the *Book of the Red Deer*, the great Gaelic scholar William J. Watson shows that there are references in ancient Scottish Gaelic poetry to 'combined hunts', that certain place names perpetuate the memory of them and that tradition connects the name of Malcolm Canmore with the ruins of a 'hunting house' in Mar, Aberdeenshire. As Watson says, 'these great hunts served the Gaelic nobles as an excellent and popular preparation and discipline for warfare; they took, in fact, the place of our modern "autumn manoeuvres".' He shows that one of the last hunting mobilizations 'was that held in Braemar by the Earl of Mar in the end of August of 1715 to cover and initiate the Rising of that year'. The great hunts 'passed with the passing of the Stuarts', and nowadays 'there are not enough men in the Highlands to make it possible to revive them'. Our annual 'Highland games' are almost the only survivals of the ancient autumn gatherings, but we still hear references in Gaelic to the 'badger's moon', following the 'harvest moon', which ushers in the time for accumulating stores of food for the winter season.

Dogs were employed in these hunts and were also used in war. A reference to these is found in the *Book of Leinster* story

'Fingal Rónain', translated by Kuno Meyer, which relates to personages in the seventh century. It tells us that the son of an Irish king visited Alba (Scotland) with fifty warriors. He found that the Scottish king 'had hounds for hares, hounds for boars, hounds for deer', while hounds were used in battle. Another story, 'The Battle of Mag Mucrime', tells of the sojourn in Scotland of the deposed king of Munster, named Lugaid, and his followers. The visitors distinguished themselves in battle and in 'assembly and game and horse race', and during the hours of leisure played with skill games that resembled backgammon, draughts and chess.

When invasions of Pictland occurred in ancient times, the nobles could raise large forces of men as they were accustomed to do in connection with their annual hunting expeditions. The Pictish system of centralized government enabled a king to mobilize an army quickly by commanding his mormaers ('sea lords') and other nobles to concentrate their forces in any particular area.

During the Viking Age, the Scandinavians might raid a district and plunder it freely, but they were not left to settle down for the winter to rest and collect food supplies and horses for their spring campaign, as they invariably did in Ireland and England. The Picts were accustomed to winter campaigning. As we have seen, they were able to attack Hadrian's Wall during the fourth century in the depth of winter. Even in Agricola's time the Caledonian and other Celtic tribes engaged in winter fighting. Tacitus says of the hardy Highlanders that they 'were accustomed to compensate the summer's losses by the successes of the winter'.

The Scandinavians were 'summer sailors' and summer campaigners. If they chanced to winter in a Pictish mainland seaport, they were not likely to be left in peace. The surrounding country was cleared of its livestock and laid waste. It was dangerous to penetrate far inland, for the men who had been mobilized for the hunting expeditions were wily and dangerous opponents and ever ready to waylay and cut down foraging parties. A Scandinavian leader who ventured to winter on the mainland coast may well have found reason to say of his opponents, as did Agricola when he addressed his army before the battle of Mons Graupius: 'We have not the same acquaintance with the localities, or the same supplies of provisions – nothing but our hands and arms, and on these we must wholly depend.' It should not surprise us, therefore, to find that in Scotland the Scandinavians had during the Viking Age fewer and smaller winter settlements than in either Ireland or England. At a later period, however, the Norsemen rented land from Highland nobles. This is shown by such surviving place names as Scatwell ('rented field') in Ross and Cromarty, and Scatdale, Argyll.

In the middle of the ninth century, King Kenneth mac Alpin had not only kept the Scandinavians at bay but had acted aggressively towards them on land and at sea. It was even possible for him to extend his rule southwards of the Forth. He certainly could never have conducted six campaigns against the 'auld enemy', the Angles, if the Norse pirates had constantly menaced the coasts of Pictland.

Kenneth appears to have cooperated with the Irish in restricting the operations of the foreign sea rovers. His son-in-law, Aed Finnliath, King of Ireland, waged war with so much success that he cleared his country of Norse settlers to the north of Dublin and Limerick. The appearance on the Irish coasts of the Danes, known as the 'Black Foreigners' or 'Black Gentiles', created a situation that must have greatly facilitated his operations, for they attacked the Norwegians, fighting

**44**

several fierce battles. They are first mentioned in 851. After settling their differences the Danes and Norsemen became allies for a period.

When in 866 King Aed Finnliath had achieved his most notable successes, two Scandinavian kings reigned in Dublin. These were Olaf the White and Ivar the Boneless. The Irish records refer to them as 'brothers', but it is more probable that they were allies and therefore simply 'blood brothers', Olaf being Norse and Ivar Danish. We find Ivar referred to as 'chief king of all northmen [Norse and Danish] in Britain and Ireland'.

Finding themselves baffled in Ireland, the Scandinavians, after composing for a time their mutual rivalries, turned their attention to the countries that were to become known as Scotland and England. A great campaign of conquest had been planned, and the 'master mind' appears to have been Ivar.

In 866, four years after King Constantine, son of Kenneth, had come to the throne, Olaf and his 'brother' Audgisl penetrated Fortriu in Pictland and took hostages in pledge of tax. They appear to have remained for some months, wasting and plundering the land, but they did not achieve any permanent success.

A curious story of dissension between the 'brothers' is given in the *Fragments of Irish Annals* of Duald MacFirbis. It tells us that in 866 Olaf (Anlaf) and Ivar both hated Auisle for secret reasons. Auisle said to Amlaeibh, after requesting freedom of speech: 'Brother, if you are not fond of your wife, the daughter of Cinaedh [Kenneth], why not give her to me? and whatever dower you have given for her, I will give to you.' At this Amlaeibh drew his sword, dealt Auisle a blow on the head and killed him. This 'daughter of Kenneth' could not have been either the daughter or the granddaughter of Kenneth

**45**

mac Alpin. Skene is wrong, therefore, in assuming that a daughter of the Pictish king had married a Scandinavian ruler in Ireland.

Some months after Olaf invaded Pictland, Ivar descended with a strong fleet on the eastern coast of England. The fact that he gave Bernicia a wide berth is of special interest. He may have expected Olaf to have overrun that area. The Picts and the Britons appear, however, to have defeated Olaf's plans in the eastern Lowlands.

According to the record of the *Anglo-Saxon Chronicle* for the year 866, the large heathen army (under Ivar) that landed in England fixed their winter quarters in East Anglia. There 'they were soon horsed' and 'the inhabitants made peace with them'.

At the time Northumbria was in the throes of civil war. King Osbert had been overthrown by the usurper Aelle, the last Anglian king of Northumbria. Mercia had suffered decline, having been similarly weakened by internal dissension. Both kingdoms had been forced to acknowledge the overlordship of Wessex, which seemed destined to become the predominant partner in a united England when the Danish invasion occurred.

In the course of five years East Anglia, Deira and northern Mercia were subdued. King Aelle of Northumbria was executed by having the figure of an eagle carved upon his back, salt being rubbed into the raw flesh. He was thus horribly tortured before he died. According to the Norse traditions, he was dealt with in this manner because he had tortured Ragnar, Ivar's father. We cannot, however, regard as sound history the Icelandic stories about Ragnar and his sons. All that seems certain in the evidence they afford is that the invaders of England were mainly Danes. King Edmund of East

Anglia, who was captured in battle, met with as terrible a death as did King Aelle, for he was tied to a tree and shot to death with arrows. Halfran was left by Ivar to continue the war in England during this the time of King Alfred of Wessex, who was to be long remembered as a great national English hero.

In 870 Olaf and Ivar were besieging Dumbarton, the Britons of Strathclyde having evidently given them much trouble, and their operations continued for four months. Evidently the defenders of Dumbarton were in the end compelled to submit because they ran short of water, the well inside the fort having 'miraculously dried up'. Strathclyde was plundered, much booty being taken in Dumbarton.

Olaf and Ivar returned to Dublin in 871, and the *Annals of Ulster* state that their fleet consisted of two hundred vessels, and that they had as captives large numbers of Angles, Britons and Picts.

Ivar died of old age two years later. Olaf fell in battle soon afterwards.

The fall of Dumbarton and the wasting of Strathclyde appears to have given King Constantine I an opportunity to extend the Pictish area of control in the Lowlands. In 872 we find that at his instigation Artgal, king of the Britons, was assassinated. The next king of the Strathclyde kingdom was Run, the husband of one of King Constantine's sisters.

From this period Strathclyde, like Dalriada in earlier times, became closely linked with Pictland. King Run's son, Eochaid, became king of the Picts in 878.

King Constantine had to contend with serious invasions. A fleet of a hundred Norwegian ships under the command of Olaf, son of Godfrey (not be confused with Olaf the White), descended on the Pictish coast, but Constantine won a victory and Olaf was slain.

**47**

During the latter part of his reign a Danish invasion occurred on the east coast. King Constantine fought a battle at Dollar, but his army was defeated and he himself slain. The Picts were forced to retreat towards 'Achcochlam' (Atholl). The king's body was buried in Iona.

According to another record, the battle was fought not at Dollar but Inverdovat, which Skene has identified with Inverdovet in the parish of Forgan in northeastern Fife. The *Chronicle of Melrose* states that the battle was fought near the 'black cave'. A cave at the East Neuk of Fife is still known as 'Constantine's cave', and it may be that it was occupied by the king at some time during this campaign.

In *Berchan's Prophecy* Constantine is said to have been a tall, fair man, and he is significantly referred to as 'the cowherd of the fold of the cows of the Picts'. He is stated to have fought four battles against the Fair Foreigners (the Norsemen) and one against 'the Britons of green mantles', a reference apparently to his operations in Strathclyde. The day of his death in battle against the Danes is given as Thursday.

Aed White-foot, another son of Kenneth mac Alpin, was Constantine's successor, but he reigned for no more than a year, dying of wounds in the Battle of Strathallan. His slayer was Giric, son of Dungal.

The next king was Eochaid, son of Run, the king of Strathclyde, and grandson of Kenneth mac Alpin. His name means 'yew warrior', and there was in pagan times a yew cult that was connected with Iona. Giric is said to have been his foster father, and he took so prominent a part in the government of Pictland that he was virtually the ruler.

Giric is credited with having subdued Bernicia and invaded the country of the Angles (Deira). According to *Berchan's Prophecy*, the power of the Strathclyde Britons was low in his time, while that of Scotland of 'the melodious boats' was high. Evidently the Scots of Argyll were strong at sea, and the custom of singing while rowing was as common in Giric's time as in that of Dr Johnson, who crossed from Skye to Raasay in a 'melodious boat', the Highland oarsmen singing in old-time fashion.

Giric was a champion of the Columban Church and is said to have relieved it of the servitude it had been forced to endure under the Picts.

An eclipse of the sun occurred during the reign of Eochaid on 16 June 885, the day of St Cyrus. Both Eochaid and Giric are said to have been expelled from the kingdom in 889.

Donald II, son of Constantine, was the next king, and he reigned for eleven years. He is referred to in *Berchan's Prophecy* as 'the rough one' who cared little for sacred relics and psalms. His reign was a disturbed one, for he had to fight against both Gaels and Fair Foreigners. The fact that he died at Forres is of special interest, because during his reign the Norsemen became very active and aggressive in the north of Scotland.

During the reign of Constantine I, Harold Fairhair had completed the conquest of the states of Norway, which he welded into a single kingdom. A number of the earls who refused to submit to him fled to Orkney, Shetland and the Hebrides, where they became leaders of pirate bands. In the summer they harried the coasts of Norway, and their depredations became so serious that King Harold fitted out an expedition and crossed the North Sea to deal with them. At the time Donald was king of the Picts.

King Harold first visited Shetland, where he slew all the Vikings who did not flee before him. Then he 'cleansed' Orkney of pirates. He afterwards plundered in the Hebrides

**49**

and on the mainland of Scotland. His operations extended southwards to the Isle of Man. Shetland and Orkney were thereafter included by Harold in his kingdom, and he appointed as first Earl of Orkney, Rognvald (Ronald), Earl of Moeri, father of Rollo, the conqueror of Normandy. Rognvald subsequently gave the Orkney earldom to his brother Sigurd Eysteinson.

Some time later Sigurd formed an alliance with Thorstein the Red, son of Olaf the White, King of Dublin. They mobilized a strong force and overran Caithness, Sutherland and parts of Ross and Moray. The Gaelic mormaer, ('sea lord') Maelbrigte Tooth, had a meeting with Sigurd at Ekkjalsbakki, which Skene located in the Grampians but Watson has shown to be Oykel Bank, Ptolemy's Ripa Alta (High Bank) at the head of the Dornoch Firth. It had been agreed that the leaders should each be accompanied by forty men, but Sigurd arrived with eighty because, according to the *Orkneyinga Saga*, he imagined that the mormaer would be faithless.

'We are betrayed!' exclaimed Maelbrigte as the Norsemen drew near, 'but let us brace ourselves and each kill a man before we all perish.'

A hard conflict ensued, and the Gaelic mormaer's force was slain to the last man.

Sigurd had Maelbrigte's head suspended from the saddle straps of his horse, but as he rode away the projecting tooth that gave the mormaer his nickname punctured the calf of one of Sigurd's legs. The wound subsequently swelled and caused Sigurd's death.

It is of interest to note that Sigurd was buried in a 'howe' at Cyderhall, near Dornoch. In 1230, as Watson has shown, Cyderhall, the modern anglicized form of 'Sigurd's howe', was 'Sywardhoth'.

**50**

Thorstein the Red, according to the saga evidence, proclaimed himself king of northern Scotland, having made peace with the Scots, but his reign lasted for only about a year. He was slain in a battle that was fought in Caithness. His mother, Aud, gave her daughter Groa in marriage to Duncan, a Caithness mormaer whose name clings to Duncansby. Then she took flight to Orkney. She and her followers subsequently settled in Iceland, which had been discovered by a Norse explorer, perhaps after hearing of it from the Irish or the Picts, for Irish hermits had previously lived in that island.

King Harold's invasion of Shetland, Orkney and the Hebrides had stimulated emigration to Iceland. Many of the early settlers were of mixed Norse and Celtic blood. As they built their houses of wood and required wood for their ships, they had, after exhausting local supplies, to import regular supplies of timber, at first from Scotland and later from Norway as well. The elm tree, which flourishes in northern Scotland and does not grow in Norway, figures prominently in the Helgi and other lays of Iceland.

King Donald II, 'the rough one', appears to have held sway in the Lowlands. He was the first king of both the Scots and Picts to be referred to as *ri alban* or 'king of Alba'. Another king named Donald, who ruled over Strathclyde, was probably his nominee and, perhaps, a near relative. After having his kingdom repeatedly ravaged by the Norse, Donald II was killed in battle near Dunnottar in the year 900.

# CHAPTER VI

# Scots and Angles as Allies

The next king of the Picts and Scots was the famous Constantine II, son of Aed and grandson of King Kenneth mac Alpin. He reigned for forty-three years (900–943) and then vacated the throne to become a monk.

Constantine was a strong supporter of the Columban church and is said to have won victories because St Columba assisted him. We are told that the king and his men 'fervently prayed to St Columba because he was their apostle and because they had received the faith through him'.

In the sixth year of Constantine's reign an assembly was held upon the Hill of Belief, near the royal town of Scone, and it was resolved that 'the laws and discipline of the faith and the rights in churches and gospels should be kept in conformity with [the customs] of the Scots'. The churchmen's chief representative was Bishop Cellach.

Three years earlier Dunkeld had suffered from a Scandinavian raid, but in the following year (904) the invaders were defeated in Strathearn, and Ivar, grandson of Ivar the Boneless, was slain. Again, the help of St Columba was cited.

When in 918 Constantine had to fight against another force of Scandinavians in Strathearn, he and his men similarly adored St Columba. They won a great victory, slaying the leader, Ottar, son of Iargna (Iron Knee), and, according to Duald MacFirbis, 'it was long after that before the Danes and Scandinavians again attacked them.'

There can be no doubt that Pictland and Dalriada prospered during the long reign of Constantine. *Berchan's Prophecy* visualizes for us a country of good cheer with fruitful trees, an abundance of corn, cattle and milk, with ale and music in plenty. The king was a hero to his people because he was fortunate in battle, and, being a very devout Columban churchman, he was regarded as a man specially favoured by God.

Like his predecessor, Constantine II held the Scandinavians in check, and he appears to have exercised considerable influence to the south of the Forth and Clyde. His brother Donald succeeded Owen as King of Strathclyde. This is the Donald, father of Malcolm, the next Strathclyde king, who is mentioned in the *Life of St Catroe* as king of the Cumbrians. He is said to have accompanied Catroe to Leeds, 'the boundary of the Northmen and the Cumbrians'.

The Danes had settled down in northeastern and central England, and when King Alfred died in 901 he was at peace with them. Alfred was succeeded by his son Edward, known to history as Edward the Elder, who in 910 had trouble with the Danes in the north and had also to deal with Viking raids in the southern part of his kingdom. In 912 his brother-in-law, the king of Mercia, died, but the widowed queen, Edward's sister Ethelfled, proved herself a worthy daughter of Alfred the Great, for she not only held the territory she had inherited but reduced Danish power by conquering strong towns and fortresses, including Derby and Leicester, while her brother extended his dominions until he subdued East Anglia. When the 'Lady of Mercia' died, Edward occupied her country and subsequently set himself to reduce Northumbria.

**53**

It is said that Ethelfled arranged a defensive treaty with the Britons and Scots. It provided that if the Scandinavians attacked one of the contracting states, the others should come to its aid. Mention is made of a Scandinavian raid in Strathclyde, but although the invaders plundered freely, they were prevented from occupying that country.

Bernicia is not mentioned in connection with this treaty. Its king, whose capital was Bamburgh, was until 912 Adulf, who had been King Alfred's friend. He was succeeded by his son Aldred, whose brother Utred was a joint ruler. They are referred to as the friends and allies of King Edward.

The Danes had never settled in Bernicia but appear to have held its king tributary for a time. Evidently the Picts were still active in this area.

About 915 northern England was invaded by Danish and Norse Vikings, who had been harrying extensively in Ireland. They occupied part of Bernicia under the command of King Ronald, and King Aldred sought the help of King Constantine, who marched southwards with a strong army that, no doubt, effected a junction with a Northumbrian force. No resistance of a serious character was met until the allies reached Corbridge. There Ronald, the heathen king, defeated Constantine and forced him to withdraw from St Cuthbert's lands between the Rivers Wear and Tees.

According to the *Annals of Ulster*, Constantine next met Ronald's army about 918 on the banks of the Tyne – apparently the Lothian Tyne. Ronald had deployed his force in four divisions, one of which lay in ambush. The Scots defeated the three that were in sight but were subsequently attacked by the fourth in the rear. Darkness brought the conflict to an end. Although the *Annals of Ulster* state that King Ronald was slain, we find that in 919 he captured York. He died in 921.

The fact that King Constantine waged war so far south is a sure indication that he occupied a considerable area of old Bernicia. Indeed, the Lothians had apparently since the time of Constantine I been dominated by the kings of the Picts and Scots.

King Edward was more than a match for King Ronald, for by 921 he compelled the Danes of Northumberland to acknowledge him as their overlord. According to the *Anglo-Saxon Chronicle*, he also received the homage of the kings of Bernicia, the Scots and Strathclyde, but it is more probable that he simply arranged a treaty of peace with Constantine, who had been in alliance with his sister, the 'Lady of Mercia'.

King Edward the Elder was succeeded in 925 by his natural son Athelstan, a proud, courageous man with golden hair, who was an ambitious statesman and a military genius. When his life's work had been completed, he was acclaimed in the *Annals of Ulster* as 'the summit of the nobility of the Western world'.

Soon after he came to the throne, Northumbria was overrun by Olaf, who is called in the records 'a King of Scotland'. Probably he reigned over the Gall-Gaels of Galloway and was influential in some of the western islands. King Athelstan strengthened his army by employing as mercenaries the pirate adventurers who at the time infested the sea coasts, and he defeated Olaf heavily at the battle of Vinheath, which became the theme of a long saga story. Olaf fled to Scotland, and he ultimately married a daughter of King Constantine, who, like Athelstan, was ever ready to avail himself of the help of foreigners to further his own ends.

In 926 King Athelstan had a meeting at Eamot, in Yorkshire, with Constantine, king of the Picts and Scots, Owen, king of Cumbria (Cumberland), Howel, a Welsh king, and

Aldred, king of Bernicia. A treaty of peace was arranged and confirmed by oaths. The *Anglo-Saxon Chronicle* would have it that Athelstan 'governed' the other kings, but when we find it stated that they 'renounced all idolatry', we cannot regard the record as other than misleading. Constantine was not a pagan, and the other kings ruled over Christian states. The thirteenth-century English writers assert that King Athelstan's allies did homage to him.

For a time the English king's hands were full in connection with the Danish trouble in the north. When Sigtrygg, 'king of the Black and White Foreigners' (Danes and Norsemen), died, his son Guthfrith succeeded him at York, but he was expelled by King Athelstan and sought refuge at King Constantine's court.

The relations between Athelstan and Constantine subsequently became strained. No doubt the refugees in the kingdom of the latter gave trouble on the English coasts and promoted unrest in Northumbria. At any rate, Athelstan must have had good cause for mobilizing a strong army and large fleet to wage war against his dangerous northern rival. He must have selected an opportune time when the pirate fleets were engaged in widespread operations, for in 934 he suddenly invaded Scotland, wasting and plundering with vigour.

According to the *Annals of Clonmacnoise*, Athelstan reached Edinburgh with his land force, but the *Chronicle of Melrose*, drawing upon English records, tells us that he crossed the Forth and penetrated to Dunfoeder (Dunnottar) and Wertermore. According to the Gaelic scholar William Watson, Wertermore corresponds to *Magh Fortrenn* ('the Plain of Fortrenn') – that is, Strathearn. Symeon of Durham says that the fleet harried as far north as Caithness.

According to Florence of Worcester, the twelfth-century

historian, Athelstan invaded Scotland because Constantine
had broken the treaty of peace, and he compelled that king of
the Scots and Picts to give him valuable gifts and to hand over
his son as a hostage. His statement that a great part of the land
was laid waste is confirmed by the *Anglo-Saxon Chronicle*,
which, however, makes no reference to a battle. Somewhat
conflicting accounts of a battle are given by the medieval
writers. According to these, Constantine was heavily defeated
in the vicinity of the Forth and compelled to surrender. He
subsequently agreed that Scotland should pay tribute to
Athelstan and his successors.

The English king is further said to have remained in Scotland for three years, during which time he subdued the western islands. Then follows the story that when King Athelstan
returned by way of Dunbar, he drew his sword and cleft a
rock with a single blow. The historian who tells this fairy
story declares that the severed rock, which could be seen by
all-comers in his day, remained as an unmistakable sign that
the Scots had been conquered and subdued by the English.
The fact that such a 'sign' was located at Dunbar indicates
that Constantine held sway in the Lothians.

King Constantine plotted to be avenged on the invader. He
formed an alliance with the Vikings of Ireland and the Hebrides, and drew on the military resources of Strathclyde. Then
in the year 937 he invaded England. A fleet of over 600 vessels had been mobilized. The *Chronicle of Melrose* makes Olaf,
Constantine's son-in-law, enter the mouth of the Humber
with his great force, but it is more probable that he entered
the Solway Firth and that Constantine's son-in-law was co-
operating with the other Olaf, son of Godfrey, the king of
Dublin.

A great battle was fought at Brunanburgh – a terrible and

lamentable battle, as a record in the *Annals of Ulster* says, and it ended in a complete victory for King Athelstan. Thousands of the invaders were slain, and among these, according to the *Chronicle of Melrose*, were five kinglets and seven earls. Florence of Worcester tells us that the conflict began early in the day and continued until evening, when Olaf and Constantine were compelled to flee to their ships. A poem in the *Anglo-Saxon Chronicle* states that Constantine, 'the grey-haired man, the old malignant', lost a son (Ceallach) in the battle and that when the fleet returned with the survivors it 'sought Dublin and Ireland again'. The battle is declared to be the greatest ever fought on English soil since the coming of the Angles and the Saxons across the North Sea. But it was not, in the purely racial sense, a battle between Englishmen and Scotsmen, for there were Scandinavians on both sides.

Eric Blood-Axe, son and successor of King Harold of Norway, appears to have settled in England after this battle was fought. He had been deposed in 935 owing to his harshness and cruelty, in which he is said to have been encouraged by his wife, Gunhild, a little woman of great beauty but ferocious spirit. His successor was King Haakon the Good, the younger son of Harold Fairhair by his mistress Thora of Moster. Harold was about seventy years old when Haakon was born, and he sent the boy to England to be fostered by King Athelstan.

When Eric Blood-Axe lost the throne of Norway, he became a Viking, harrying the coasts of Scotland and England. King Athelstan made friendly overtures to him and offered him a portion of Northumbria on condition that he would defend it against all invaders. Eric accepted this offer and consented to be baptised as a Christian. He is said to have been as greatly hated in Northumbria as in Norway, and he was once, perhaps twice, expelled from that state, but he returned again. In the end he was slain while on a pirate expedition, either in 950 or 954.

Athelstan died in 939 and was succeeded by his half-brother Edmund I.

King Constantine II, having grown old and frail, vacated his throne in 943 in favour of Malcolm, son of Donald II, and he became the abbot in the St Andrew's monastery of the Culdees (*Cele dei*, 'friends of God'). According to the *Annals of Ulster*, he died in 952.

King Malcolm mac Donald, in the seventh year of his reign, raided England as far south as the River Tees, taking numerous prisoners and many herds of cattle. According to a Scottish chronicle, Constantine is said to have planned this raid. He asked Malcolm to be allowed to resume the kingship for a week to avenge himself upon the 'auld enemy'.

Edmund, the Anglian king, had early in his reign to deal with a rising in the Danelaw, the parts of Anglo-Saxon England in which Danish customs and laws were observed, which made common cause with Northumbria. He was able to suppress the rebels, and after harrying Cumbria, he gave all that country to Malcolm on condition that he would be his ally on land and sea. This was in 945, and in 952, according to the *Annals of Ulster*, a battle was fought by Foreigners (Vikings) against the Scots, Britons and English. The *Annals of the Four Masters* say that the Foreigners were victorious.

Malcolm I (Malcolm mac Donald) is referred to in *Berchan's Prophecy* as the 'Battle Fury', apparently a reference to the Irish war god Bodb Dearg. During his reign the Vikings were very active around the coasts. There was also trouble in Moray, where a native rising occurred under the leadership of Cellach, but King Malcolm suppressed it, Cellach being slain in battle. In 954 Malcolm was killed in Moray 'by treachery', and he was buried in Iona.

Indulf, the next king, was a son of Constantine II, and during his reign of about eight years (954–62) there were conflicts with Vikings on the east and northeastern coasts of Scotland. A record tells us that the fortress of Eden was evacuated, but whether this refers to Edinburgh, Carriden (Cair Eden) or Eden in Fife is quite uncertain. Nor do we know who the occupants of the stronghold were. A force of Scandinavians was defeated in Buchan, and in another conflict at Invercullen, King Indulf was killed. *Berchan's Prophecy* speaks of him as a good king and a worthy son of Constantine's, referring to him as 'the Aggressor'.

King Dubh (Duff), his successor (962–66), was, after a reign of about four years, slain by treachery at Forres. Evidently there was much unrest in Moray, where Viking raids must have been frequent.

King Culen (966–71), son of Indulf, was operating in Strathclyde when he met his death at the end of his short reign. According to one source, he had wronged a young woman, and her father, Amdarch, set fire to the house in Abington, Lanarkshire, in which the king slept, and he perished in it, although he may have met his end in battle with the Britons of Strathclyde.

King Kenneth II, son of Malcolm, who next came to the throne, reigned for about twenty-four years (971–95). He was a contemporary of the English King Edgar, who inherited a kingdom that had been greatly strengthened and pacified by that great ecclesiastical statesman St Dunstan. Danelaw had been subdued and the coasts were well guarded by Anglian fleets. The Danes were allowed to retain their laws in Yorkshire and Northumbria, and Dunstan employed Danes in posts in the church and state. Trade with continental Europe was in a flourishing condition, and a revival of religious activity was accompanied by a revival of learning.

A treaty of peace was arranged between Kenneth and Edgar. According to the *Anglo-Saxon Chronicle*, Edgar held a great conference at Chester, where he met six kings, and they all covenanted with him that they would be his allies by sea and land. The twelfth-century English historians assumed that the other rulers acknowledged Edgar as their overlord, but this was a manifest exaggeration. Edgar is represented, however, as anxious to conciliate the king of Scotland, for he is said to have presented to him a hundred ounces of gold, many robes and ornaments, and many precious stones. He also 'gave him Lothian', which may simply mean that he recognized King Kenneth's claim to the eastern Lowlands of Scotland, which, since the battle of Nechtansmere, had been mainly under Scoto-Pictish control. Bernicia had shrunk to small dimensions, and its Anglian under-kings were merely Lords of Bamburgh. With the exception of Athelstan, no Anglo-Saxon king had for a long period been able to make his power felt in Lothian, because the Danish kingdom in northern England formed a buffer state between it and the territory ruled by Anglian kings.

The kingdom of Kenneth II extended from the Tweed to the Pentland Firth. Strathclyde was a vassal state, and although there were Norse settlements in Caithness, its rulers appear to have acknowledged Kenneth as overlord.

Although King Harold Fairhair of Norway had formally annexed Orkney and Shetland, he had secured no hold upon the mainland. This is made manifest by his recorded dealings with Torf Einar, Earl of Orkney. When Einar slew Halfdan Halegg, a son of the Norwegian king, that monarch came west with a strong fleet. Einar fled to Caithness, where he was safe, and Harold had to make terms with him, simply imposing a fine for his son's death.

Earl Thorfinn, son of Torf Einar, married a daughter of Duncan, Earl of Caithness. One of his sons, whose name was Skuli, was made an earl by King Kenneth. This roused the jealousy of his brother Liot, who raised an army and drove Skuli out of Orkney and Caithness.

At this time Macbeth, perhaps the ancestor of the Macbeth who became King of Scotland, was mormaer ('sea lord') of Moray. He provided Skuli with an army, and a fierce battle was fought in Caithness. Liot won a victory and Skuli was slain. According to the *Orkneyinga Saga*, after that time there was great enmity between the Scottish king and Liot. Macbeth was sent into Caithness with a strong force, but although Liot set up a brave defence he was mortally wounded and died soon after the battle, which had been quite brief.

Hlodve, another son of Thorfinn, next became Earl of Orkney. He married Edna, daughter of the Irish king Kiarval, and their son was Sigurd the Stout. It appears that Hlodve had become mormaer of Caithness under the Scottish king, for when he died he was buried at Hofn in that county.

In the fifteenth year of Kenneth's reign a Danish invasion of Dalriada was repulsed, no fewer than 140 prisoners being hanged. Iona suffered severely, however, for on Christmas night in 986 it was plundered by Danes, who slew the abbot and fifteen monks. The *Annals of Ulster* tell of the slaughter in the following year of 360 Danes who had plundered Iona. Their violation of the Columban holy place must have created widespread horror not only among the Celtic peoples in Scotland and Ireland but also the Christianized Norsemen of Dublin and the Hebrides.

**62**

Sigurd, Earl of Orkney, was increasing his power in the north. He had inherited the mormaership of Caithness but appears to have regarded that area as a personal possession. Norway was kingless from 970 till 995, being ruled by Earl Haakon, to whom Sigurd owed no allegiance. When we find Sigurd raiding Sutherland, Ross and Moray, it becomes evident that he did not regard himself as a subject of the Scottish king. He was an ambitious man, and later we find him aspiring to become the king of Ireland.

Macbeth, Mormaer of Moray, was succeeded by Findlaech (Finlay), son of Ruadri and father of the Macbeth who was to become king of Scotland. He attempted to curb the growing power of Sigurd but suffered defeat in the Battle of Skidmoor in Caithness. Sigurd had the aid of Vikings from Iceland, including the sons of Njal (Neil), a descendant of an Irish family, as his name indicates. This famous Icelandic 'Neil' is celebrated in the famous *Saga of the Burnt Njal*.

King Kenneth II appears to have been assassinated in Angus in 995, but the circumstances attending his death are obscure. His slayer is said to have been Finella, daughter of Cuncar (Connachar), the hereditary mormaer of Angus. Her grievance against the king was that he had slain her son. Her name is a rendering of *Finnghuala* ('white-shouldered').

A war of succession was waged after Kenneth's death. Constantine the Bald (Constantine III), son of Culen, came to the throne, but after a reign of only a year and a half (995–97) he was slain in battle at the mouth of the River Almond. His opponent, Kenneth, son of Malcolm I, was also slain.

Kenneth III, son of Dubh, was the next king, and he reigned for about eight years (997–1005), with his son Giric II as co-ruler. They were both slain in battle at Monzievaird, between Crieff and Comrie. Their opponent was Malcolm

II, son of Kenneth II and grandson of Malcolm I, who was the great-grandson of King Kenneth mac Alpin. Kenneth III himself was a grandson of Malcolm I and the first cousin of his slayer's father.

According to John of Fordun, King Kenneth II had decided that the complicated system of succession should come to an end and that after his time a son should succeed a father. He was therefore hated by the princes of the royal line, and it may have been owing to their plottings that he was slain by Finella. His son, Malcolm II, appears, however, to have been the type of king of whom Scotland was in need, for, despite the bloody start to his reign, he proved himself a great ruler and general in a time of peril when the very existence of Scotland as an independent nation was being threatened by the Danes.

# CHAPTER VII

# Triumph of Celtic Scotland

Three great events in the history of northern Europe occurred in the early part of the eleventh century. In 1014 the question of the sovereignty of Ireland was decided by the defeat of the Norsemen at the Battle of Clontarf. In 1016 King Canute (Cnut) completed the conquest of England, which became part of the kingdom of Denmark, and in 1018 King Malcolm II won the decisive Battle of Carham, shattering the Anglo-Danish power of Northumbria and finally incorporating the entire Lowlands into the Scoto-Pictish kingdom. Malcolm subsequently secured overlordship of Orkney and Shetland. When Thorfinn, during a visit to Norway, was asked by King Olaf to recognize his suzerainty, that famous Earl of Orkney, the most powerful of his line, answered, 'I cannot well pay you homage, as I am already an Earl of the King of the Scots and his vassal'.

Olaf forced an unwilling verbal allegiance from young Thorfinn, who did not, however, regard it as binding. Olaf himself was soon afterwards dethroned by Canute, who added Norway to his dominions.

Although all hope of Norse supremacy in Ireland was shattered by the Celtic victory of Clontarf, the Norse kingdom of Dublin remained intact, as did also other Norse colonies.

The 'fair strangers' and 'dark strangers' who elected to remain in Ireland were finally incorporated in its Irish-speaking population. Their language perished so completely that only a few place names like Waterford and Wexford have survived, a fact that emphasizes how perilous it is to be guided by linguistic evidence alone in dealing with the migrations, settlements and fusions of races.

England was united finally by King Canute. He suppressed the old rivalries of Mercia, Northumberland, Wessex and East Anglia and 'drew closer than of old the ties which bound the rulers of these great dependencies to the Crown'. Anglo-Saxon England began to feel the benefit of the unity that had been the aim of the dynasty of Alfred and had long been employed in Scotland north of the Forth under the centralized government of Pictish kings whose political ideals were perpetuated by King Kenneth mac Alpin and his successors.

In Ireland, on the other hand, King Brian's vision of a united kingdom was not shared by the rulers who followed him. There was no lack of national feeling, but that unifying influence was countered by a conservative adherence to national traditions of government. King Brian fell at Clontarf, and Mael Sechnaill held the high kingship until his death in 1022. Then for half a century Ireland was again a country of petty states, as had been, except for comparatively short intervals, Anglo-Saxon England prior to the Danish conquest.

It is quite manifest to the unprejudiced mind that the racial question has no real bearing on the question of the system of government. Celtic Ireland could not achieve the permanent union, under a strong centralized government, that was accomplished by a Celtic king in Celtic Scotland, and Anglo-Saxon England required a Danish conqueror to weld its rival states into one and give its people peace and prosperity.

66

There can be no doubt as to why Scotland gave England and Ireland the lead in the science of government and why great kings like Oswald and Oswy, who had been educated in Scotland, became men of large vision. In Scotland the Caledonians and their successors, the Picts, had in measuring their strength against Rome learned by experience that national independence is to be achieved by national unity. The Pictish system of government by kings to whom the mormaers were subject made possible Scotland's notable resistance to Scandinavian aggression and also the establishment of a united Scotland from the Cheviots to Shetland under the Celtic kingship of Malcolm II, who is referred to in the *Annals of Tigernach* as 'the honour of all the west of Europe'.

In *Berchan's Prophecy* we find Malcolm spoken of as 'the florid one', as a 'good king', 'a heavy battler of a strong people' and a 'destroyer of foreigners'. Of special interest is the fact that he is said to have been 'a Leinster woman's son'. Apparently Kenneth II had contracted a political marriage with a princess of the Irish kingdom of Leinster, which maintained an alliance with the Norse kingdom of Dublin. Earl Sigurd's mother, Edna, was likewise an Irish lady of high birth, the daughter of the Irish king Kiarval (Cerball), and it may be that she was related to the queen of Malcolm II.

King Malcolm II began to reign in 1005 and he died in 1034. He came to the throne as the victor of a family feud, having, as we have seen, slain his second cousin Kenneth III, known as 'the Grim' or 'the Graeme', and his son Giric II.

The year of his accession was a terrible one in England, for, according to the *Anglo-Saxon Chronicle*, that unhappy country suffered from a terrible famine. Ethelred the Unready (or the Heedless), who had begun to reign in 979, had to wage a terrible struggle with hordes of Scandinavian Vikings, and he

**67**

endeavoured to enlist the help of the Normans by marrying Emma, daughter of Richard I, Duke of Normandy, and sister of Richard II, the grandfather of William the Conqueror.

Svein, king of Denmark, and Olaf Tryggvisson, who was to become king of Norway, took part in these raids, and enormous sums of money were paid to bribe them to make terms of peace. Ethelred attempted to form a standing army by employing Scandinavian mercenaries, but he was unable to keep these adventurers in hand. During an interval of comparative peace that was secured by heavy bribes as 'tribute', Ethelred consented to the wholesale massacre of Danes, and it took place on St Brice's Day, 12 November 1002.

King Svein raised a great army to avenge this act of treachery, and the war of real conquest then began. The Danes swept like a forest fire into East Anglia, sacking towns, plundering holy places, slaughtering young and old without mercy, and laying waste the country. The famine of 1005 brought their operations to a halt, but in the following year they were ravaging in Kent and Sussex.

Malcolm II must have had hopes of adding Northumberland to his kingdom, for in 1006 he crossed the Tweed with a large army and swept southwards. He did not pause at the strong fortress of Bamburgh, in which Waldeve, the aged earl, had shut himself, but pushed on to Durham, which he besieged. He paid dearly for his rashness. Utred, the elder son of Waldeve, mobilized a force of Northumbrians and, attacking Malcolm, defeated him heavily. According to the *Annals of Ulster*, the Scots lost many good men. We gather from Symeon of Durham that Utred had the heads of many of the slain Scots set up on stakes around the walls of Durham. The interesting detail is given that, according to the fashion of the time, the Scots nobles had their hair braided.

In 1016 King Canute, son and successor of King Svein, had completed the conquest of England. Ethelred died a natural death, and his natural son, Edmund Ironside, after arranging a treaty of peace with Canute, died suddenly. Perhaps, as has been suggested, he was poisoned by the enemy.

Earl Utred had espoused the cause of the Danes, but Canute, who could not trust him, had him put to death. He was succeeded in the earldom by his brother Adulf, who, according to a chronicle preserved by Symeon of Durham, was both cowardly and timorous. Fearing that King Malcolm II would seek to avenge the disaster of 1006, he granted him the whole of Lothian in order to secure peace. Thus, according to an Anglian record, Lothian was once more ceded to Scotland. As we have seen, it had already been 'given' to King Kenneth II by King Edgar (959–75). Apparently some of the English chroniclers have 'protested too much' in this connection.

In 1018 King Malcolm again invaded the earldom of Northumbria, the northern boundary of which had for long been the Tweed. His army included a force of Britons under the command of Owen the Bald, the vassal king of Strathclyde. A decisive victory was won at Carham, and, according to a record given by Symeon of Durham, 'almost the whole people, including their nobility, between the Tweed and the Tees, were slain'. The *Annals of Durham* tell us that this disaster was heralded by the appearance of a comet and that among the slain were eighteen priests who had foolishly taken part in the war. Bishop Aldhun died from grief a few days after the battle, and his see remained vacant for about three years.

The peace that was subsequently arranged by mutual agreement could not have left King Canute unconcerned. Rodulfus Glaber, the eleventh-century historian, cannot be ignored in this connection, although his records may be otherwise somewhat confused and embroidered with fable. He tells us that Canute went northwards with a large army to subdue the Scots but found Malcolm strong in arms and resources and a good Christian. After a time, owing to the intervention of Richard II of Normandy, Canute arranged a friendly treaty with Malcolm and became the godfather of the son of that Scots king. But this final touch is evidently fable, for Malcolm II had no son.

Attempts were subsequently made, by tampering with the records, to establish the claim that Malcolm submitted to Canute and became 'his man'. Edward I, in his letter of 1301 to Pope Boniface VIII, asserted that Scotland had not only been held 'in subjection' by King Canute but also by Edmund Ironside, Ethelred, Edward and Edgar, and after Canute's time by Harold and 'Harthacnut'. When, however, Saxo Grammaticus, the Danish churchman, wrote his history of Denmark in the thirteenth century, he did not include Scotland among the kingdoms that were subject to Canute. Nor does Canute himself in a letter that he wrote when returning to Denmark from Rome during his pilgrimage of 1031. Florence of Worcester, the twelfth-century English historian, who drew on earlier sources, and the *Chronicle of Melrose* make no mention of a submission of King Malcolm to King Canute. The assertion that Canute was overlord of the Scottish Lothians was, however, made in Norway when King Olaf the Saint was called upon to acknowledge Canute as his superior, but it appears to have been nothing more than a diplomatic fiction, and this may account for the saga references in the same connection. The *Anglo-Saxon Chronicle*, of which different versions have been preserved with interpolations and omissions, especially for the eleventh century, makes Canute, on his return from Rome in 1031, visit Scotland to receive the submission of King Malcolm and also of two other kings, named Macbeth and Jehmar, but adds that Canute held Malcolm's allegiance for 'a little while only'. This confused statement disagrees with that which refers to the representations made to King Olaf of Norway, who was dethroned in 1028 and died in 1030, the year before Canute visited Rome. King Canute died in 1035.

Much light was thrown on the Lothian problem by the Gaelic scholar William Watson in his *Celtic Place-Names of Scotland*. He showed that a number of significant place names indicate that many Britons survived between the Forth and the Tweed during the Anglian period and that from about the middle of the tenth century the Gaelic language became current in this area. There is evidence of the settlement of Gaelic-speaking communities in what are now known as the Border counties and of proprietors with distinctive Gaelic names, including Macbeth of Liberton and Gillomichael. The latter is mentioned by Symeon of Durham, who knew that the name meant 'Lad of Michael' but considered it should have been 'Lad of the Devil' on account of Gillomichael's lack of respect for the Anglian churchman. No doubt Gillomichael was a Columban. Gaelic personal names occur in the Allerdale district of Cumberland in an English document of the eleventh century referred to by Watson.

King Malcolm II seems to have completed the Scottish conquest of Lothian by expelling the Anglian lairds and farmers and giving their lands to Gaelic-speaking people. The present-day Scots of the Border counties are, as MacNeill and other Celtic scholars agree, descendants of the Gaelic-speaking colonists who were settled in the Lowlands during the tenth and eleventh centuries.

During the interval between his defeat near Durham and

the Battle of Carham, King Malcolm II found it necessary to attend to the welfare of the northern part of his kingdom.

The extent of the area controlled by Sigurd, Earl of Orkney, has been greatly exaggerated by some writers. He inherited the earldom of Caithness and thus became the nominal subject of the king of the Picts and Scots. In 995 he was visited by Olaf Tryggvisson, who had been living the life of a Viking and had been converted to Christianity by a hermit of the Scilly Isles. Olaf was proceeding to Norway to claim the throne and caught Sigurd at a disadvantage. He compelled the earl to become a Christian and swear allegiance to him, and he took away as a hostage Sigurd's son Hund ('Whelp'). When, several years later, Hund died, Sigurd, according to *St Olaf's Saga*, 'showed no obedience or fealty to King Olaf'. Olaf perished in a famous naval battle in the year 1000.

About 995 Sigurd defeated Finlay (Findlaech), father of the famous Macbeth and Mormaer of Moray, in the Battle of Skidmoor in Caithness. It has been asserted that Finlay was independent of Malcolm II, but he appears to have married that king's sister. Macbeth is referred to in the *Chronicle of Huntingdon* as the nephew of Malcolm.

Malcolm II must have come to an agreement with Sigurd, to whom he gave one of his daughters to be his second wife. Sigurd gave no further trouble to the Scottish king but proceeded to plot with Sigtrygg, the Norse king of Dublin, and Gilli, the Hebridean earl, to conquer Ireland and become its high king. Before he set out on his Irish expedition, which terminated in his defeat and death at the Battle of Clontarf, Sigurd sent Thorfinn, then a boy of five, to the Scottish court to be cared for by his grandfather, King Malcolm II.

When the Scottish king heard of Sigurd's death, he appointed Thorfinn Earl of Caithness and Sutherland, and chose good men to rule the land for him. It is manifest, therefore, that when Sigurd married the Scottish princess, he must have acknowledged King Malcolm as his overlord in Caithness and Sutherland, and that was why Thorfinn subsequently declared to the king of Norway that he could not be that monarch's 'vassal for service', being 'an earl of the Scottish king', to whom he owed fealty.

Malcolm seems also to have established his power over the Inner Hebrides, for in *Berchan's Prophecy* he is referred to as 'voyager of Islay and Arran'. The Strathclyde kingdom, which extended into Cumberland, was ruled by his grandson Duncan, son of Crinan, the powerful lay abbot of Dunkeld, and Malcolm's daughter Bethoc. Owen the Bald, who led the Britons in the Battle of Carham, died in the same year (1018).

In the thirtieth year of his reign (1034), Malcolm II died after being wounded in a conflict with the Moray family. A feud connected apparently with the right of succession to the Scottish throne had long been smouldering in the north. In 1020, Finlay the Mormaer had been slain by his nephews, the sons of Maelbrigte, and nine years later (1029) we find mention of the death of Malcolm, son of Maelbrigte, who had claimed to be king of Scotland. In 1032 Gillacomgain, another son of Maelbrigte, who is referred to as mormaer of Moray, was burned with fifty followers, and in the following year Malcolm II slew the grandson of Boite, son of Kenneth III. Gillacomgain had married Gruoch, a daughter of Boite, and that lady subsequently married Macbeth. To many she is known as Shakespeare's 'Lady Macbeth'.

It was evidently because Duncan, son of Crinan, the Atholl noble, had been selected by Malcolm as his successor to the throne that the Moray branch of the royal family were in revolt. They had been previously loyal to Malcolm.

**73**

Duncan I succeeded his grandfather, Malcolm II, as king of Scotland and reigned for fewer than six years (1034–40). The *Annals of Tigernach* state that he was killed by his subjects at an 'immature age'. It is certain he was a younger man than Macbeth. Duncan's father, Crinan, was killed in a battle 'between Scots' in 1045 – that is, five years after Macbeth came to the throne.

Duncan had married a sister of Siward, the Dane, and, when he died, his two sons, Malcolm and Donald, were mere children. It is apparent, therefore, that we should dismiss from our minds the Shakespearean vision of an aged and grey-bearded King Duncan, who made 'Lady Macbeth' think of her father as he lay asleep. Tradition has nothing to tell us of his personal appearance, but it affords us glimpses of his Danish ally and brother-in-law and of his Celtic kinsman and rival. According to Henry of Huntingdon, Siward was 'almost a giant in stature, strong of hand and strong of mind', while in *Berchan's Prophecy* Macbeth is pictured as a tall man with a ruddy complexion and light yellow hair, and referred to as the 'furious red one' but yet a 'generous king' who made Scotland feel 'joyful', quite different from the stage Macbeth.

Duncan may well have incurred the displeasure of his more influential subjects by introducing into his court his wife's Danish relatives. Like his grandfather before him and his son after him, he had dreams of adding to his kingdom the remnant of the old Anglo-Celtic state of Bernicia. He was probably assisted by his Danish relatives when in 1039 he raided northern England and laid siege to Durham. According to the *Annals of Durham*, Duncan was defeated by the besieged and sustained great losses. A record preserved by Symeon of Durham states that many of his cavalry were slain and that most of his infantry perished during his confused retreat.

About a year later Siward avenged this disaster, for Symeon of Durham tells us that he defeated and slew Adulf, son of Utred, and made himself earl of the Northumbrians.

King Duncan's fate had, however, been sealed. The losses he had sustained in his Durham campaign involved a serious drain on his military resources, and he was unable to suppress a revolt that broke out in the northern part of his kingdom. The leader was Macbeth, and Duncan appears to have been slain in a battle that was fought in the vicinity of Elgin.

Macbeth at once seized the throne, to which he had a double claim as the nephew of Malcolm II and the husband of Princess Gruoch. He reigned for seventeen years (1040–57), and, according to *Berchan's Prophecy*, Scotland prospered and was 'brimful' under his rule. A record in the *Chronicle of Melrose* says that the seasons during his reign were 'fruitful'. Commerce must have flourished, for Macbeth acquired considerable wealth. No doubt this was due in no small measure to the suppression of Scandinavian piracy in the North Sea after Canute had united England, Denmark and Norway under his sway.

Macbeth's supremacy was threatened, as has been indicated, by a rising in Atholl in 1045 under the leadership of Crinan, Duncan's father, who was, however, defeated and slain. Nine years later Earl Siward invaded Scotland with a fleet and a land force of mounted men. The English records assert that he put Macbeth to flight and captured a great deal of booty. Both Florence of Worcester and William of Malmesbury credit him, however, with the conquest of Cumbria, the old kingdom of Strathclyde, over which he set as king Malcolm Canmore, son of Duncan. Henry of Huntingdon tells us that during this campaign Siward's son Osbarn was slain. When the news of his death was carried to the earl, he asked if the young warrior had been wounded in front or behind. 'In front,' he was told. Then Siward exclaimed, 'I rejoice because of that, for I would regard my son or myself worthier of no meaner death.'

Four years earlier (1050) Macbeth had been on a pilgrimage to Rome, and there he is said to have scattered money 'like seed', his beneficiaries being the poor. Earl Thorfinn visited Rome about the same time, and it has been suggested that he accompanied Macbeth, the two men being close friends and allies. He first went to Norway. King Magnus, whom he had consistently refused to serve as a vassal, was dead and, having left no son, was succeeded by King Harold Hardruler, the only surviving descendant in the male line of Harold Fairhair. The earl was well received by the new king. He afterwards visited King Svein in Alaborg and the Emperor Heinrek in Saxland. From the latter he received horses that enabled him to ride overland to Italy. If Macbeth accompanied him, it is possible that the two friends were on a diplomatic as well as a religious tour.

Thorfinn's relations with his first cousin, King Duncan I, are somewhat obscure. The *Orkneyinga Saga* states that after King Malcolm II died the throne was seized by Karl or Kali Hundason, who wished to remove Thorfinn from the earldom of Caithness, appointing Moddan in his place. Thorfinn, however, expelled Moddan by force, and thereafter the King of Scotland came north with an army and a fleet of eleven warships. Thorfinn won a naval victory in the Pentland Firth, and King Karl fled to Breida fiord (Broad Firth = the Moray Firth). Thorkel, Thorfinn's ally, slew Moddan in Caithness and afterwards joined forces with Thorfinn in Moray. A battle was fought at Torfness (Tarbatness) on the southern side of the Moray Firth, and King Karl was defeated. Thorfinn is said to have subsequently raided Scotland as far south as Fife. Then he returned to Caithness, where he spent the winter. If Karl Hundason was King Duncan, Thorfinn may have been cooperating with Macbeth, his mother's first cousin.

When Thorfinn died he possessed, according to the *Orkneyinga Saga*, eleven earldoms in Scotland, including that of Galloway. The fact that during the early part of Macbeth's reign (1041–42) he invaded England, suggests that he was not friendly to Siward. In Orkney he gradually increased his power until he became sole earl. The year of his death is uncertain, but if he lived longer than Macbeth he may have come to an understanding with Malcolm Canmore (Malcolm III). Thorfinn is sharply characterized in the *Orkneyinga Saga* as 'a man of very large stature, uncomely, sharp-featured, dark-haired and sallow and swarthy in his complexion . . . a most martial-looking man of great energy; greedy of wealth and of renown; bold and successful in war and a great strategist.' His mother, as we have seen, was a Scot; his paternal grandmother was an Irishwoman.

Earl Siward died in 1055, and his successor in the earldom of Northumbria was Tostig, son of Godwin, the nominee of Edward the Confessor (son of Ethelred the Unready and Emma, the Norman lady).

In 1057 Malcolm Canmore defeated Macbeth in battle at Lumphanan. Macbeth subsequently died of wounds and was buried in Iona. Lulach, his wife's son, was recognized in the north as his successor, but was slain in the following year in Strathbogie. According to the *Annals of Tigernach*, Lulach was killed by treachery. He, like Macbeth, was buried in Iona.

When Lulach fell, Malcolm Canmore became sole King of Scotland.

# CHAPTER VIII

# $\mathcal{A}$ EUROPEAN KINGDOM

The reign of this third Malcolm, known as Canmore (Big-head), was of enormous importance to the course of Scottish history, although not entirely through his agency. The time was critical. A new age had begun – the dawn of a fresh and stable civilization in Europe. The arrival of what we call feudalism meant the achievement, by a Christendom struggling to recover from centuries of barbarism, of a reasoned, intelligible and universally applicable pattern of government and of law and of property. On the spiritual side, the organization of the church, which had remained largely intact through the disorder of the Dark Ages, took on the discipline and strength of a truly organic vitality. On the secular side, there developed the code of chivalry – an almost mystical idealization of mundane living scarcely less potent in moulding men's lives than religion itself. Spiritual and secular together made a complete and singularly compact whole, a unity of culture and order that as a driving force was irresistible by lesser orders and cultures.

It was perhaps a temporary unity in the sense that there quickly grew up within it ideals of individual nationality. But that individual nationality could still regard itself, on occasion, as having the whole moral weight of the new feudal community behind it. Thus France, from one point of view no more than a part of European Christendom, was yet, from another, the distinct nation that was the centre and head of the medieval economy. That curious doubling of national power sped the Normans in their invasion of England. The south crumbled, not merely before the Normans but before the full impact of the new Europe. And the Norman Conquest brought that power within striking distance of Scotland. The north had barely withstood the attacks of the south under the Saxon kings. Now, under Norman conquerors and the rule of a race far stronger and far more daring than the Saxons, the south should have overwhelmed the north. Scotland, a primitive Celtic state still lacking complete unity, was in fact due to be Normanized by force or else to suffer the heartbreak of alternating struggle and repression under partial subjection. That neither of these fates overtook Scotland was sheer accident; it would be truer to call it a miracle, since nothing else could have averted catastrophe. And the accident, or miracle, was the marriage of Scotland's king.

Malcolm III was married twice, first to Ingiborg, who died in 1069, leaving three sons, one of whom would later become Duncan II. Malcolm then married for love a penniless princess who was also a beautiful woman. The amazing luck of this marriage was that the bride was, in addition, the sister of the legitimate heir to the English throne, a fugitive with her brother from the conqueror of Hastings. And, as if that were not enough, she was further a European by upbringing, reared at precisely one of those courts of Europe where the feudal pattern of order and culture was held in most respect and dignity. Finally, she was a woman of conspicuously strong character and determined energy. Malcolm's Margaret was, in fact, the first of Scotland's memorable queens; the first

**79**

woman in history to lay hold of the Scottish destiny, lifting it out of one course and setting it down in another. And it is St Margaret (she was canonized in 1250 by the Roman Catholic Church) who is, from the historical as from the human point of view, the dominant figure on the throne.

Not that her husband became a cipher. Far from it. He was a bonnie fighter, and accordingly he fought. One immediate result of his marriage was that his hands were strengthened, as the brother-in-law of the English heir apparent, for action against the Norman usurper, whose strength in the south and attempted encroachments on the north were a constant menace. Malcolm's reign is one long record of thrustful raids across the Border and strategic defence and retreat on his own side of it. He fought William the Conqueror, and after him William Rufus, with zeal and some apparent success, until in 1093 he and his eldest son met their deaths, only a few days before the death of Queen Margaret, in asserting Scottish independence against an insulting English denial of it. But actually he left his kingdom with diminished limits and to some extent a divided people, for his death was a death in defeat, and it was followed by a little war of succession between his elder sons and his brother, which vexed the country and to some extent slowed its progress for nearly thirty years until his youngest son, David, reached the throne in 1124.

Queen Margaret's influence was much more far-reaching. What she (and later her sons, of whom she had six, as well as two daughters) did was to give to Scotland gradually, peaceably and in amity much the same injection of the great new civilization of medieval Europe that the Normans gave to England, but suddenly and violently at the point of sword and lance. England was conquered in the process, but Scotland remained inviolate. And that, although it was doubtless only possible by the martial prowess and strong protection of her fire-eating husband, was really St Margaret's doing. Without her, the northern kingdom could not have been able, in less than a century, to rank as a universally known and respected province of united Christendom.

Her great work for Scotland was manysided. She was a woman of extreme, almost fanatical, piety, but she laid the foundation of reform in the church and fostered the learning that emanated from it. As part of her encouragement of the minor but cumulatively important arts of life, she made Scottish existence less bleak and bare, and brought good manners and taste to the court so that it became a place with some reputation for luxury and refinement. The fugitive incomers of rank from the south to whom she gave assistance and shelter were ready instruments for adding this leaven of culture to the Scottish lump. They helped, for instance, the process by which Scotland became an English-speaking instead of a Gaelic-speaking country, but in particular they helped to provide the kingdom – especially the war-ravaged Lowlands – with experienced men of rank who knew better than the Gaelic lords how to deal with the peculiar dangers of the new era. Above all, perhaps, she gave Scotland a heightened status and exactly the access to prestige that it needed.

Scotland's kings had been mighty men, but only in their own kingdom and on its Irish and Scandinavian fringes. Yet the world of that kingdom, to the newcomers from Europe and to the continent from which they came, might have seemed a mere unenlightened darkness on the outskirts of Christendom – but for Margaret. She was patently a very great woman in her own right, undeniably the kinswoman not only of kings but of universally acknowledged saints, and herself steeped in the odour of sanctity. And she was the king

**81**

of Scotland's queen. Neither her crown nor her kingdom, nor yet her descendants, could be treated with disrespect.

Accident again, as well as heredity, helped to make it inevitable that her sons should carry on her policy and keep the face of Scotland turned towards the new Europe. One result of the little war of succession that broke out on the deaths of Malcolm and Margaret was that their youngest sons had to be kept out of harm's way. So Alexander and David, who were still small boys, were sent to the court of their sister Maude or Matilda, who had married the English Henry. They received there a most useful training. That court was not so much English as Norman-French, and the Normans, as we have seen, had not only brilliant political and administrative genius but also the most enriching kind of contact with the intellectual leadership of France. Thus the two boys grew up in a stimulatingly European atmosphere, and when the time came they were prompt and energetic to spread in Scotland the best of contemporary modern thought.

Meanwhile in Scotland the little war of succession was brought about by Malcolm's brother Donald Bane (meaning 'fair'). On the death of Malcolm and Donald's father, Duncan I, at the hands of his rival, Macbeth, Malcolm had taken refuge in England while Donald had retreated to the Hebrides. During his exile, Donald Bane was exposed to Celtic culture, and after Malcolm succeeded to the throne in 1058 he began to nurse a hatred of Margaret's increasing influence on the Scottish court. After Malcolm's death in 1093, Donald III seized the throne at the age of sixty-two and attempted to reverse the anglicization of the court. His position was soon threatened, however, by Malcolm's son Duncan, who had been trained as a Norman knight during his father's exile in England.

An invasion led by Duncan, with the backing of an English and French army, dethroned Donald in 1094, but Donald regained the throne when Edmund, another of Malcolm's sons by Margaret, killed Duncan II, his son by Ingiborg. Another of Malcolm and Margaret's sons, Edgar, then had Donald blinded and imprisoned in 1097. Donald died three years later and became the last Scottish king to be buried on Iona.

Edgar took the throne in October 1097 but was practically a dependant of William Rufus and later Henry I of England. Shortly after his accession, Edgar's kingdom was threatened by Magnus Barelegs, king of Norway, who brought a considerable fleet into western waters and forced Edgar to cede 'all the isles around which a ship could sail', including Kintyre.

In his ten-year reign (1097–1107) Edgar pursued a pro-English policy, settling the first English knight in Lothian. He died unmarried and was buried in Dunfermline. He was succeeded by his brothers, Alexander and David. As it happened, they ruled together for seventeen years, the senior as the titular Alexander I, King of Scots North of Forth, the junior David as Earl of Lothian and Strathclyde. The arrangement proved to be less dangerous in practice than it promised to be, chiefly because of David's ability to sustain himself by Norman aid without becoming its pawn.

Certainly the two brothers respected each other's strength and resources. There is no evidence of discord between them during their joint rule, and their common policy of civilizing Scotland and preserving its independence made persistently for the kingdom's consolidation.

David is the more memorable of the two, history sometimes accounting him the greatest king Scotland ever had and his reign the most beneficial to the country at large. It was undoubtedly marked by statesmanship of a high order. When

he became David I, King of Scots, in 1124, he had already
served a seventeen years' apprenticeship in south Scotland.
He had brought to the Lowlands a practical appreciation of
the Norman civil organization and a backing of Norman
nobles to aid his introduction of it. He established some of
them in the lordless and lawless lands of Strathclyde and Lothian, where they assured him of effective military support
against rebellion and invasion. These lands thrived under this
control – it was to David's excellent government that Lothian
owed its increasing importance as the commercial and political centre of Scotland. He continued his saintly mother's gen-
erosity to the church. It was partly a political move – through
a church attached to the crown by gratitude and interest the
crown achieved a hold on the country not otherwise attain-
able. But David's establishment of bishoprics throughout almost the whole land gave to the church a complete and vital-
izing organization that it had never known under the Celts
and that brought Scotland completely within the pattern of
ecclesiastical Christendom. And the richly endowed abbeys
of monks that he planted up and down his kingdom became
more than religious centres; they were also centres of learning
and the civilized arts, not least that of skilled agriculture.

There was a parallel to this modelling of ecclesiastical affairs
in David's handling of the lay polity. He set up the great state
offices common to all feudal administrations. The country
came to know something like uniformity in law. There came
into existence the first of the trading burghs, either by confirmation or deliberate establishment. And David extended this
ordered aspect of the feudal pattern to the wayward north.
Gradually, and for the most part peacefully, the old Celtic in-
stitutions took on the new feudal shape – the former
mormaers became earls, and the subordinate landowners bar-

ons. The king occupied himself with the remaking of Scotland, and of a Scotland independent and standing on its own feet, not a state subservient to the Norman south.

The process was conducted with what was, considering the time, a surprising minimum of violence. Not that David was a particularly peaceable king. He inherited his share of the paternal fighting genius, and his reign knew war and certainly one smashing defeat at English hands. But it was England more than Scotland that suffered the ravages of his war-making. Although he followed the traditional policy of grasping at Northumberland and Cumberland, it was a civil war in England that provided his opportunity, and the dynastic claims of his niece, the Empress Maude, his pretext for interfering in English affairs. In the circumstances Scotland escaped the worst of the usual counterattack and consequences of intervention of that sort. But it had its price. It cost David the death of his promising son, Henry, who was the pivot point of his English policy and had the makings of a good king; and in a later reign it exacted a brief payment of Scottish subjection to England. These English possessions that David had attached to the Scottish crown were to be a burden in subsequent years. But for the moment Scotland itself knew something like peace and flourished accordingly, a country that had voluntarily accepted the new civilization of Europe and in consequence was counted a kingdom among the other kingdoms of Christendom.

Henry's premature death meant that a boy of twelve succeeded David on the throne, and the new Scotland learnt that even under feudalism the country's welfare depended on the strength and ability of its kings. The accession of Malcolm IV (Malcolm the Maiden), David's grandson, was the signal for certain too newly fused elements in the kingdom to seek to fly apart. There were revolts and internal dissensions. David's gains at English expense had to be surrendered, and Malcolm passed on a critical situation to the brother who succeeded him.

This was William I (William the Lyon), not a minor as Malcolm IV had been, but hardly a judicious monarch – rash, impetuous and something of a fool, in his younger years at least. He may have shown alertness to recover some of Scotland's lost possessions across the Border, and certainly his alliance with the rebellious English heir gave him an excuse for his raids. But it was not alertness that led him into the foolish skirmish at Alnwick when he attempted to take the Castle. He was taken by surprise by an English force, captured and taken to Henry II at Northampton, with his feet shackled beneath the belly of a horse. Henry, who had that very day finished his public penance for the murder of Thomas a Becket, must have been soothed by the captured of the Scots king. William was imprisoned at Falaise Castle in Normandy, where the following December he was obliged to accept the terms of the Treat of Falaise under which he was to acknowledge the sovereignty of England over Scotland, including himself, his kingdom and the Scottish church. William was discredited at home on account of the treaty, and until Henry II's death it cost him trouble with rebellious subjects in more than one part of his domain. Then in 1189 Henry was succeeded by Richard I, who, perhaps wiser than his father, restored Scottish independence for a good round sum, thereby financing one of his pet Crusades and securing the north's friendliness during his absence.

There are two things worth noting about this transaction. One is that the money paid to Richard seems to have been raised by something like a general assessment laid on Scotland, a possible fact that has been held to prove the existence of some sort of well-developed constitutional machinery in the kingdom. The other is that the tax, if tax it was, proved a first-class investment, yielding a valuable dividend. And that was peace – peace between Scotland and England that lasted for more than a hundred years and was the foundation for the great century of the Alexanders, which came to be looked back upon as Scotland's early Golden Age.

It was that in truth. Scotland in the thirteenth century moved through rapid political, commercial and intellectual advance. It was a time of steady progress towards a unity, a fullness of life, and a strength that have perhaps never been known since. And this growing sense of nationhood marched with a serene sense that Scotland was nevertheless part of Europe. Scots scholars, Scots soldiers and Scots merchants were familiar up and down the continent. If the wave of progress touched all Europe at this period, Scotland was in many ways on the crest of it. For the quickening of life was not confined to the ruling class; it could be seen and shared in by all free men – in the new towns, the new churches, the new castles and the new prosperity. Berwick, for instance, was one of the chief trading towns of Northern Europe.

And this stir of activity was general. The main part of the Lowlands – naturally rich provinces – had the most of it. But the Gaelic north was not left out of the vivifying stream. There is proof in the fact that it had nine of the eleven bishoprics that had been established at the beginning of the Middle Ages, nine centres of the new civilization. That civilization, too, was spreading north and west; a sort of national expansion was pushing out the remaining Viking settlements. Alexander II pacified Argyll by force of arms, and Alexander III crushed the last serious Norse aggression in the famous

Battle of Largs. And in the south there was peace, fostered by political marriage and a preoccupied England whose self-absorption the Alexanders used as an opportunity, not to raid over the Border but to build up and strengthen the rule of peace and order on their side of the marches. After a long winter of preparation and promise, Scotland was entering upon a summer of fulfilment.

But it was a brief summer, and it ended in tragedy, with consequences from which Scotland never fully recovered. The fine qualities of the Alexanders were doomed to lack inheritors; their line was to fail. There had been anxiety on this score in the time of Alexander II. He had married first the sister of the English Henry, and second the daughter of a powerful French house, but his only son was born of that second marriage and born late in his reign – so late that before the birth a boy cousin of the king had been ceremoniously acknowledged presumptive heir in order to ensure the succession. A prince was born, however, to succeed to the throne at the age of eight as Alexander III.

Like his father, this Alexander also married in England – Henry's daughter this time – and a child of that marriage became queen of Norway. Yet before Alexander was out of his prime, while he was still in the full vigour of early middle age, he was without an immediate heir. His wife, sons and daughter were dead, and his only descendant was that daughter's daughter, the infant princess who was to be the ill-fated Maid of Norway. The danger of this situation was appreciated, and in 1284 a solemn assembly was summoned at Scone to settle the succession on this months'-old child. It was simply a precaution, for in the following year Alexander married again, also like his father, in France, a young queen and reputedly beautiful.

Then the blow fell. On a March night in 1286, when there was a fierce storm raging over the Firth of Forth, King Alexander was completing a Council of State in Edinburgh while his lovely Queen Yolette awaited him over the water at Kinghorn. He would go to her, although the night was wild for travelling and there was counsel at hand to dissuade him. He went. And when morning came a well-loved King of Scots lay dead at the foot of a cliff where his horse had stumbled. Scotland's sovereign was a motherless babe on the other side of the North Sea, and there had dawned for Scotland an interregnum that was irresistible temptation to Edward Plantagenet, watching greedily from England.

# CHAPTER IX

# FROM KINGDOM TO NATION

Scotland was an anxious country in that spring of 1286. For although the obvious things in a child queen's minority were promptly done, although a regency was set up to carry on the government, there was evidence of other claims to the throne and no lack of trouble brewing. It came quickly, from that boy cousin whom Alexander II had named as his successor before the birth of Alexander III. That boy was now an old man, but powerful as the Lord of Annandale, and his claims were supported by a son who was an earl, with an earl's backing. For two years intermittent war and peace reigned in the southwest of Scotland, and the strife was watched by another boy, who was to become the great Robert Bruce and a King of Scots. The old Lord of Annandale was his grandfather.

Then events took a new turn. The child queen's father, Eric of Norway, happened to be considerably beholden to Edward of England, and in 1289 he sent commissioners to that monarch to discuss the affairs of the little girl who was Norway's daughter, England's grandniece and Scotland's queen. Edward invited the Scottish regents to send representatives to this conference and began to jockey for position. He got it. It transpired that he intended to marry his son to the Maid of Norway – a foreshadowing of that Union of the Crowns that was not to take place for more than three centuries yet. The Scots had no objection, and a marriage treaty, safeguarding the ancient liberties of Scotland, was successfully drafted. This readiness of the Scots to accept Edward's intention need not be too surprising. The English king was the Scots queen's granduncle, for one thing; for another, he was the feudal overlord of those of the Scots nobles, mostly Norman in ancestry, who held lands in England as well as in Scotland; and finally, the north had been at comparative peace with the south for the best part of a hundred years. Further, the proposed marriage had advantages for Scotland as well as for England, and if it had come about, in fact, the history of these islands might have been less stormy and the history of Europe very different. But history does not deal in 'might have beens', and the whole scheme perished with the death of its centrepiece.

The Maid of Norway sailed for Scotland in the autumn of 1290 but never reached her kingdom, dying in Orkney on the voyage. Mystery surrounds her death. No account of it has survived, and there have been, in consequence, suspicions of its actual circumstances – although foul play seems to be ruled out by the fact that a body apparently went back to Norway for burial that King Eric acknowledged as that of his daughter. At any rate no more is heard of the tragic little Margaret, a Queen of Scots who never reigned and who never saw or was seen by Scotland.

The fat was now in the fire in earnest. Pretenders to the throne multiplied – there were thirteen of them, all told – and although half the lawyers of Europe were ready to pronounce an opinion on the succession problem, the nearest (and largely self-appointed) arbiter was Edward Plantagenet, something of a lawyer himself but still more of an opportunist. And when Edward came to the Tweed to deliver judgment, he came with an army and the announcement that he was the rightful feudal overlord of all Scotland – 'Lord Paramount of Scotland', as the schoolbooks had it. This large claim left the Scots thunderstruck, as it well might, but the answering of it plainly needed a counter-argument as strong as Edward's army, and in any case it was matter for a king, of whom they had none – yet. So Edward proceeded to arbitration, unchallenged in his mighty role, and finally paused at the short leet of the 'Competitors', whom law and discretion had now reduced to two.

They were both descendants of David I. One was John Baliol (with lands in Picardy, incidentally), the other old Bruce of Annandale. It was a close thing between these two, for although Baliol came of an elder line, he was at a further remove (and that by female descent) from their joint ancestor. But Bruce, although old, was a strong man. The younger Baliol was weak, and weakness was what Edward Plantagenet wanted in a King of Scots. He gave the award to Baliol, who duly did homage for his kingdom and was crowned at Scone as King John in 1292. But Scotland, not at all deceived, called him the 'Toom Tabard'.

There was, indeed, emptiness within his robes of royalty. The new king took slight after slight from the hands of his English puppet master, until at last the accumulation of humiliations goaded him into rebellion. But Baliol rebelled, as a weak man always does, with more fury than force. He had a paper alliance with Philip of France and no popularity at home either to win or keep an army at his back. In 1296 Edward, who had been waiting for the chance, moved north and crushed him, achieving the ghastly Sack of Berwick on the way and returning to England with an ex-king at the tail of his march. Among the plunder sent ahead to London were

92

three chests full of the Scottish royal records and that Stone of Destiny that was to rest for seven hundred years under the chair in which British monarchs are anointed and invested at their crowning.

Edward had, to all outward seeming, done his work well, as befitted a great soldier and crafty statesman. But although he had declared Scotland to be no longer even a kingdom but merely a northern extension of England, and although there were English garrisons in the Scottish strong places and an English viceroy over all, he had in fact set in train a march of events that was to establish Scots independence more strongly than ever. His war with Baliol was over, but his war with Scotland had only begun, and it was to last more or less continuously until 1328. After six uneasy twelve-months the Peaceful Century had dissolved in a blaze that was to take thirty-two years' quenching and bring out of the ashes at the last an exhausted Scotland indeed, but also the first of Europe's nations, the unity not merely of a kingdom but of a whole people in arms in a common cause.

The two men who were chiefly responsible for that transformation were first Wallace and then Bruce. These are two names that resound throughout Scottish history, although there has until recently been an unaccountable tendency to regard Wallace as the patriot and martyr, and Bruce as the somewhat shifty strategist who waited until Wallace's work was done and then forged the weapon he had left into a brilliant instrument of personal power that took him to the throne. That point of view does scant justice to Bruce, who in fact as a young man put national interests before family claims and fought in a weary war for a feckless king, who saw futility for what it was and bided his time, without wholly laying down his arms, and who then, when that time came, took leadership in both hands and won against odds that were, by all the rules, impossible. Bruce was more than a fighter, strategist, leader and statesman – he was a hero.

The tale of Wallace in any account of Scotland must be soon told, for although he inspired all Scotland he was never a reigning king. In any case, not much, beyond his one rousing victory and his one smashing defeat, is known of him. He was a country gentleman, the second son of a laird in what was later called Renfrewshire – his name, *le Waleys*, which has a root meaning of 'Welsh', suggesting Strathclyde – and he was one of a group of Scottish liberators at first more notable than he. But he was a fighter and a leader with a general's head, and he became conspicuous in a series of raids on English posts prior to the battle of Stirling Bridge. That gave Scotland a first taste of triumph and lent such spurs to the rising that there was even an invasion of northern England. But it drew down on Scotland the might of Edward himself, and the next year, at the head of a powerful army, he caught Wallace at Falkirk. The defeat was resounding, a blow that broke up the main Scottish force and introduced a period of scattered warfare over most of Scotland, with Wallace a will-o'-the-wisp raider who was still feared despite the increasing English occupation of the country. In 1305 he was captured – tradition says betrayed – and hauled to London. Edward was afraid of him. Although Wallace had broken no oath of allegiance to the English king, for he had taken none, he was awarded the death of a traitor and hanged, drawn and quartered according to the pet Plantagenet formula. Scotland had a martyr.

That was Edward's mistake. For Wallace's martyrdom strengthened with a fiercer hate the new Scotland that he had been instrumental in bringing to birth. And that was the

Scotland whose people – the common people – were ready to fight, not for their feudal lords but for their country. It was the first hint of modem democratic nationalism, the birth of a nation. It appeared first in Scotland probably because there was one big difference between the feudalism of Scotland and the feudalism elsewhere. The Scots had never been serfs in any systematized sense, nor had Scotland any tradition of slavery such as Rome had bequeathed to the rest of Europe. And the manner of St Margaret's inoculation of Scotland with the feudal order – the absence of any forced assimilation of what was alien to the native character – had preserved the native independence. It was the common people of that sturdily free and independent character who ultimately won the war against England. They found leaders in the great barons and bishops who resented English dominance. They eventually found a hero king, but they rallied first to one who was neither baron nor bishop, nor yet a king, for Wallace, younger son of a small and far from wealthy country laird, stood close to the land and the people and could call to them to defend it in a language they understood. His leadership and martyrdom did the rest. And it was this new Scotland that was more than half made when Bruce set out to lead it – and completed the process of transformation.

His career during Wallace's lifetime needs some survey. His grandfather, the rival of Baliol at Edward's arbitration, had died in the year of the 'Toom Tabard's' first rebellion, and his father, an easy-going man, had succeeded to the crown claim but had accepted Edward's terms, where he was to stay, more or less, until his death. (The Bruces held lands in England.) But the young Robert seems to have had other ideas, although he must have been in an awkward position between family loyalties and the watchful Plantagenet eye. To join

Wallace's camp was to fight for Baliol, and therefore against his own father's rights to which he himself was heir. Yet he was 'out' in the western rising – although he missed Stirling Bridge – and there were significant English raids on the Bruce lands of Annandale. Later he was one of the Scottish Guardians in Baliol's name, apparently sinking family claims once more but falling foul of the Comyns (Baliol men) in the process. That quarrel was to have a sequel. Then later still, and probably in disgust at the handling of the Scottish cause by the Baliol party, and no doubt conscious of the futility of a struggle waged under divided leadership, he made some sort of peace with Edward – outwardly, at any rate. He was head of his family by that time, for his father had died in 1304. But there is evidence of a curious pact between him and a certain sagacious and patriotic Scots bishop who was looking to the time when Edward of England would be succeeded by a weaker man in the person of his son.

Then in February 1306 came the violent quarrel that is known to everyone as the start of Bruce's main career – the stabbing of John Comyn (the 'Red') in a Dumfries church. What led up to this event cannot now be known with any certainty. There is a quite probable story of an anti-English agreement between the two leaders that Comyn betrayed to Edward, but reason boggles at accepting Comyn's death as a deliberately planned murder. He had a secondary claim to the throne and to that extent certainly was Bruce's rival. But a violent riddance of set purpose in this fashion would have been the move of a fool. The murder itself raised the powerful house of Buchan against Bruce; its sacrilege threatened to rouse the church, one of his strongest allies in any rising, against him; and both together were a challenge to Edward for which Bruce was not quite ready. He was no fool. The

**96**

crime was passionate, then, but not cold-blooded murder. Even so, the deed was done, and a lesser man would have surrendered or fled the country. Bruce had himself crowned at Scone.

The drama of this act still stirs the imagination. It was a hurried, almost a furtive, crowning, for Edward was furious and his garrisons held the Scottish strongholds. All those who could attend it were there: representatives of the church, for Bruce had received absolution for the Comyn killing and a bishop anointed him; a handful of barons, mostly from north of the Forth; and most gallant of them all, a sister of that head of the house of Fife, then a prisoner in London, whose traditional right it was to crown Scotland's king. She was the wife of a Comyn, but she rode from Buchan to fulfil her family's coronation right. When the ceremony was over King Robert I faced his task. Against him he had the might of England, so strongly entrenched in his kingdom that he was hard put to it to find safe soil to stand on. At his back he had, in the spring of 1306, a mere handful of men, but they grew – Edward's ravages in Scotland had engendered a vengeful determination that fed recruiting. All over Scotland the men of the church – patriots before they were priests – contrived to preach his cause. But a full fighting force could not be created in a matter of months. Actually, three months after the crowning, what army Bruce had was scattered by an English surprise attack near Perth. The king was on the run with a few followers, harried in the north by avengers of the Comyn killing, to disappear finally for a winter of wandering and hiding in the isles of the west, which invites parallel with the plight of Prince Charles Edward four centuries later.

The grim winter it had been on the mainland he discovered on landing at Carrick from Arran in the spring of 1307 –

that historic landing at the summons of a flare that had been lit, not by the scout sent ahead to test Carrick's safety but by heather burners doing their routine spring job. Bruce came back not only to danger but to personal tragedy – three brothers executed, his wife and child and sisters taken captive. He had no heir, and his queen was in prison. His death would have been the end of everything, and his army was hardly even a troop. It looked like ruin – by all reasonable standards it should have been ruin. But Bruce was in his own country, his lieutenant and friend, young Douglas, the 'Good Lord James', was not far from his, and both men were born leaders. The king in particular must have had enormous personality. They are largely legendary accounts of him at this time that have come down the ages, but they tell much the same story – of a man not handsome, although of powerful physique, and with a singular charm and gentleness in his manner. One of the most striking pictures of him is of a king in hiding, at the lowest ebb of his fortunes, reading a French romance aloud to his few followers on the shores of Loch Lomond while waiting to cross to a precarious safety. No wonder men followed him.

They followed him now, through some breathless weeks of kindling excitement. It began with the famous 'Douglas Larder', when they surprised the English garrison of Douglas Castle at church, ate the enemy's Sunday dinner in the castle itself, and then wrecked it and its stores in a great blaze that made a heartening story for the rest of Scotland. It went on for seven years of brilliant guerilla warfare and desperate but heady adventure, which with an entire book to itself would still be only half told. Bruce was lucky in one respect early on in this career, for old Edward died in the summer of 1307, and the son who succeeded him as Edward II was not quite the man his father was. Nevertheless he was a most formidable adversary, and the war went on. It moved through brushes and skirmishes and small pitched battles; now with short respites, when Edward was preoccupied, which Bruce used to crush civil war in odd corners of his own kingdom; now with invasions in force, before which Bruce retreated dexterously, only to turn and harry the enemy's cumbersome army on its return march; and always with a running accompaniment of brilliant individual feats of arms, like the steady recovery of the Scottish strongholds – Linlithgow with its portcullis jammed on a farmer's cart while Lothian men hurtled through the opening to fall on a surprised garrison, or Edinburgh with its thirty men and a scaling ladder like flies on the wall of the Castle Rock in a triumphant night raid. The end of it all was that Scotland was almost entirely won back, although a handful of Lowland castles, including Stirling, were still under siege, and the people were a nation united in one cause under a great leader who was about to prove himself a great general. But the country below the Forth had been laid waste by the sore ravage of war and was nearly exhausted. One smashing defeat – and all that had been regained would be lost again. Instead, there was Bannockburn.

That battle and its result are almost too well known to be written about here. It routed the greatest English army that Scotland had seen, set the seal on Bruce's kingship and forever established the Scottish cause. But it did not end the war. What was yet to be won was the formal recognition of Scotland's independence. That did not come until the Treaty of Northampton in 1328, and it might not have come even then if Edward II had not been deposed in favour of his fifteen-year-old son, Edward III. The fourteen years' interval was filled with alternate war and truce, but the fighting now was mostly in the north of England, where the Scots raids grew ever more daring and more aggressive. English counter-invasions became increasingly expensive and increasingly futile. They found no army to fight with and a deserted, famine-stricken land to march through. Bruce was strategist until the end. But these years held more than war; they marked a further and final stage in the development of Scotland's king. He had been a great guerilla leader and a great general. He had still those qualities when the need arose, but now he revealed himself also as a great statesman.

The manifestations were many. His idea of putting his brother on the Irish throne – often held to be the sign of an overweening ambition – was sound policy. A Scottish ally on the English flank, if it could have been, might easily have saved three centuries of recurrent war. It was not to be, but Bruce's one great failure was never his fault. His statesmanship is seen again in the fact that despite all his successful raids over the Border he never thought to claim a Scottish right of possession by conquest over the north of England, as some of his predecessors had. Few men of his time so clearly saw the Border as the natural and inevitable boundary of the two countries. Then in his relations with France and still more with the popes of his day – and Rome was indeed a power at that period – he was continually and brilliantly the statesman. He was discreet and not too optimistic with France as a potential ally against England, and with Rome he was so reasonably and so intelligently stubborn that his refusal to let excommunication weigh in the balance against Scottish independence became a just and inescapable criticism of Rome's policy. And he strove, when fighting would let him, to repair the destruction of his country's war-torn districts, as he sought also to rebuild the structure of government that had fallen to pieces in thirty trying years. He has been accused of strengthening the future power of the barons at the expense of the crown by lavish grants not only of forfeited estates but also of the crown's own lands to his followers. Certainly his successors suffered from these gifts, but Bruce, with war-crippled revenues and an impoverished country, had nothing else with which to reward men who had served him – and Scotland – faithfully and well. It is significant that while he reigned, the rivalries of the great nobles were held in check, and that a parliament that he summoned in 1326 was the first to include burgh representatives.

It was his reign, too, that produced the memorable – but not nearly well enough known nor highly enough valued – Declaration of Arbroath, that amazing medieval document that is Scotland's Charter of Liberty and a magnificent state-ment of a nation's right to govern its own affairs as a free country. It contains one tremendous passage that puts passion for liberty above even allegiance to the Crown:

'Through the grace [runs a translation of the original sono-rous Latin] of Him who woundeth and maketh whole, we have been freed from so many and so great evils by the valour of our Lord and Sovereign, Robert. Like Judas Maccabeus or Joshua, he gladly endured toil, pain, the extremity of want and every danger to save his people and kingdom from their enemies. By reason of his desert as of his rights, the Provi-dence of God, the lawful succession which we will maintain with our lives, and our common and just consent have made him our King, because through him our salvation has been wrought. If he should give up our cause and yield us to Eng-land, we would cast him out as the enemy of us all, and choose another king who should defend us, for so long as

**101**

only a hundred of us stand, we will never yield to the domin-
ion of England. We fight not for glory nor for wealth nor
honour, but for that freedom which no good man surrenders
but with his life.'

Finally, Bruce was careful to secure his dynasty, in a way
that promised future peace, by arranging the marriage of his
son to the sister of the English Edward III. All that is the
record of Scotland's greatest king. The other great king,
David I, had built a kingdom; Robert I saved a nation. And
having done it, he died – of leprosy, a ghastly disease that
grew out of years of hardship – and left as heir a boy of five
who was to grow up a weak man and a foolish one.

After the glory of his father, David II is a wretched anticli-
max. Certainly trouble came to a head long before he was of
an age either to make it or deal with it. Dissension followed
hard upon the appointment of a regent. It was fomented by
Edward III, with a son of John Baliol as pawn in his treaty-
breaking, and by 1332 Scotland and England were at war
again. Things went ill for the Scots without their old leaders,
and by 1334 the young David and his queen were in France
for safety and the Plantagenet grip was strong once more on
Scotland. But the Scots found a leader in young Robert the
Steward, nephew and heir presumptive of the absent David.

Edward III began England's Hundred Years' War with
France. Scotland managed to repeat something like the guerilla brilliance of Bruce's earlier years, even to individual gallantry in arms – like the stand of 'Black Agnes' at Dunbar –
and by 1341 the country was safe enough for David and his
queen to come home. But two years later he led an army into
England in the French interest and fought a crazy battle that
left him Edward's prisoner. And a prisoner – in some comfort

**102**

– he remained for the next eleven years, until Edward thought it politic to sell him back for a crushing ransom, a truce and a trade agreement.

Scotland got the worst of that bargain – a king spoiled by the luxury of the English court, extravagant, impulsive, given to jaunts to London (his English queen had stayed in the south) and with a persistent leaning to England and things English that took him near, in the end, to blackest treachery. There was more than one flare of rebellion against him in Scotland, and it was after one of these outbreaks that David, in 1363, negotiated a secret treaty with Edward that bought redemption of his troublesome ransom at the cost of surrender of Scottish independence and reversion of the Scottish succession. The Scots Parliament never knew the worst and was so bluntly scornful of what it was allowed to know when David sought to sound it that the king dared go no further with his planned betrayal. He lived on, an encumbrance to his country, until 1372, leaving Scotland still free – although that was through no effort of his – but nearly bankrupt.

The man who succeeded him, his nephew, Robert the Steward, had done much for Scotland under David's misrule and proved himself a true enough grandson of Robert Bruce in doing it. His link with the great Robert was on the distaff side. On the other he brought a new family to the Scottish dynasty. He was the first of the tragic line of Stewarts.

# CHAPTER
## X

# THE ARRIVAL OF THE STEWARTS

The Stewart line succeeded to the throne in a bleak time. The most vital thing left in the country was a fierce nationalism; the country itself was a wreck. 'Postwar reaction' has a grim enough meaning for our own age, which has known two world wars. The Stewarts' Scotland had known a far longer and far more exhausting struggle. And the task of recovery, of reassuring revived nationhood, was hindered by almost every conceivable complication.

There was, to begin with, the immediate legacy of weakened kingship. David's travesty of a reign had unleashed the forces of greed and disunion, to say nothing of treachery, within the kingdom. Outside, able to strike easily at the country's wealthiest and most vulnerable provinces, lay England, far superior in manpower, much richer and still territorially ambitious – always a potential foe even when the ink was drying on the peace treaties. Moreover, there was the beginning, in the Stewarts' time, of a crumbling in the medieval background. The flooding energy at this time of Christendom was beginning to ebb all over Europe. The power and position of the church itself was about to weaken. And striking through that increasing confusion, adding to men's uncertainties, came the Black Death.

All these shocks in combination tended to loosen the old social framework. They also provided an opportunity to re-cast the states thus made fluid in a new and definite mould, better adapted to changed circumstances. But that required vision and farseeing idealism in a country's great men, and in Scotland, the nobles, by training and by the exigencies of im-mediate needs, were not notably idealists. They were rather men of action, exponents of a personal and businesslike prac-tical materialism that saw private advantage and the further-ing of land-grabbing enterprises in a weak kingship and a state of fluctuating law and order. Strong kings could have taught them otherwise, and strong Stewarts sometimes did – while they lasted. But – and this was in some ways a decisive complication in the Stewart period – the fatal ill-luck of their house made them a sequence of young kings, in intervals of minority during which baronial intrigue undid the best of their mature work. The two longest-lived of the Jameses – and it is significant that they were the most memorable – barely reached their forties; only three of the eight early Stewarts died in their beds, and two of these had broken hearts. It was to the testing rule of this Scotland – this Scot-land of grim present fact and menacing future possibility – that there succeeded, in 1371, a man who was too worn-out to take hold of his problem.

Robert II had given his prime to coping with the conse-quences of David's follies and to begetting a considerable progeny. When he came to the throne in his mid-fifties, his faculties were failing and his health was poor. He reigned for nineteen years as little more than a figurehead, a wise, kind-hearted but broken old man whom his nobles more or less ignored in arranging their warlike diversions. Had England not been occupied overseas they would almost certainly have

**105**

brought down on the country the very foreign war that Robert wanted to avoid. As it was, by sundry Border raids and an early variety of 'war sport', which visiting French knights apparently enjoyed, English counter-invasion was all too quickly provoked, and for a time it was virtually full war again between the two countries. Then in a supervening truce the old king died, to be succeeded by his son John in 1390.

The new king's name had such unlucky associations that he changed it, and it was as Robert III that he was crowned at Scone. But he could not change his frailness, his age and his lack of vitality. This Stewart, lamed in early manhood, had too long accustomed himself to a semi-invalid's share in the world's affairs, and coming to the throne in his fifties, like his father, he was that father over again in all but his sire's memory of a vigorous youth and prime. The reign, however, opened promisingly enough. Robert III was anxious for peace, and negotiations with England proved fruitful to that end. In the ensuing few years a brief balance was struck between England, Scotland and France, and not only political and social but also trade relations improved between the two Border neighbours. But inside Scotland matters were very different. There was constant dissension and something like a threat of civil war. The real ruling strength was in the hands of the Earl of Fife, the king's brother, who had been created Duke of Albany, and in 1399 his intriguing for power backed an anxious parliament's doubts about the king's fitness to rule. Robert was virtually deposed and made no attempt to retain his royal prerogatives. The business of government passed to a Council General, the nominal head of which was the heir to the throne, the Duke of Rothesay, but the real controller of which was Albany.

The main events of this regency, which lasted for a quarter

of a century, stand out from a stormy enough background – of baronial Border raids, renewals of the English war and Scots expeditions to France in aid of an ally. First came Albany's direct clash with Rothesay, the heir, and that prince's somewhat sinister death in Falkland Castle. Then came King Robert's frightened dispatch of his remaining son, James, a boy of ten, to the safety of the French court and the capture of the prince and his ship off Flamborough Head by English privateers. The young prince was sent to the Tower of London. That was followed by the death of the old king in 1406, which, with the capture of the new, settled Albany firmly in the Scottish saddle. And in the Albany fashion Scotland was ruled until chance and English policy let King James come home, in 1424, from his southern prison – a man grown, with some hard memories behind him, and at his side a bride of the English blood royal. The drama of a splendid effort to bring back peace, good government and a revitalized kingship to a country wasted by war and war's aftermath had at last begun.

It must have seemed, to an expectant Scotland, the red letter opening day of a new age when King James and Queen Joan rode over the Tweed to take possession of their kingdom. The Scots had lacked a vigorous ruler for close on a hundred years. Now they had one. James was twenty-nine and in the full flush of manhood – physically hardy and skilled in warlike exercises, accomplished in the graceful arts, a poet who had wooed and won a deeply loved princess (he is credited with the composition of *The Kingis Quair*, a collection of poems, passages of which praise Joan's beauty), a statesman who had pondered in exile the affairs of government and determined on his management of them. He was almost the ideal prince of his time – wise, able, just, strength-

**107**

ened in his ruler's purposes by deep religious sincerity and the profound Stewart sense of kingship. There were in his accession all the makings of a great reign.

While he lived that promise was steadily fulfilled. He had sworn to make 'the key keep the castle, the bracken bush the cow', and he kept his oath. In 1424 he had come to a wrecked kingdom. By 1437 he had transformed and set solidly in the way of betterment every major activity of the national life. He disciplined nobles, church and people, breaking the threatening power of the first, reforming the second and legislating beneficially for the third. He taught his barons to respect the treasury, restoring the wealth and the power of the crown, which had been looted of lands and revenues under the regency. He took church reform to the length of challenging the pope and won the encounter. And trade, agriculture and the arts and crafts responded to his lawmaking, through a parliament that did not escape the king's ideas of reform. Abroad, he kept the peace while enhancing his country's international prestige. He revived the old link with Norway and steered a shrewd course through the precarious intricacies of relations with France and England, marrying his daughter to the dauphin without provoking dangerous English enmity. And then, a bare thirteen years after the beginning, came the end – grim, violent, brutal.

The king had made enemies. He could hardly avoid it, tackling the task he had set himself. But James had his full share of the Stewart impatience, and in him it was reinforced by a naturally abundant energy. In achieving his purpose he had been a man in a hurry and sometimes a man with small scruple. Before he had reigned a year he had struck at the Albanies, and there were hangings. Then, in 1427, following on trouble in the Highlands, he had summoned the great men of the north to a parliament, arrested forty of them and tried and hanged three with some speed. Later still, a forfeited inheritance ranged one Sir Robert Graham against the king. He is a fanatic figure, this man, oddly lit in Scottish history by the flame of an insane hate. He had appeared in open enmity and been banished, but in James's last year he had found fellow conspirators in men who were kin to, and ostensible friends of, the king. They broke in on him at the Blackfriars' monastery in Perth, where he was keeping Christmas with the court, a band of armed men against one unarmed, trapped in a cellar like a beast in a stall, and struck him down.

Story has made that brutal murder vivid – this and that warning unheeded by the king, messengers denied audience, then the sinister rattle of arms outside the chamber where he talked with the queen and her ladies, Kate Barlass holding the door with an arm through the boltless staples while James dropped to the vault, a wild confusion of search when the killers burst in, and death by fifteen wounds in a dark struggle that could have only one end.

The queen and the king's newly strengthened law took a terrible vengeance, for the murderers died, a month later, by torture. But James I was dead, to his people's 'dule', and his heir was a boy not seven.

The succeeding twelve years were filled with a tale often enough told in the Stewart century – the relapse of one king's building up of security into the anarchy of another's minority. The young James was the legal source of power, and there was struggle for this wardship, with the Douglases, serenely arrogant in almost sovereign possession of two-thirds of south Scotland, looking tolerantly on. Queen Joan married again, not very strategically, and found herself forced out of a controlling share in affairs. Then the house of Douglas suddenly

**109**

became vulnerable through the death of its head, and the Crichton and Livingstone factions, which had been fighting for possession of the king, saw their chance in collusion. There was the ugly business of the Black Dinner, when the two young Douglas heirs, invited to enjoy young James's hospitality in Edinburgh, went to their deaths there. The affair was none of the king's planning – his guardians were responsible and the inheriting Douglas who benefited by the murder may have been privy to it – but there was blood between the crown and the house of Douglas in consequence. The check to the family's power was only temporary. In a few years, through a judicious marriage and triumphant defence of the Borders against renewed English attack, its wealth and its prestige were as high as ever. But by that time the young James was in his first manhood. The French marriage that had been arranged for him was solemnized, and in that year of the wedding he took power into his own hands as King of Scots.

James II was very much the son of his father. Lacking some of the paternal accomplishments, he possessed all the paternal energy of mind and body and the same passion to maintain Scotland's freedom, build up her prosperity and ensure her peace, both within and without. He inherited much the same sort of task, except that Scotland's prestige ranked even higher in Europe in his time than in his father's and needed less effort to keep it there. James's marriage to Mary of Gueldres, who was a woman of spirit as well as of beauty, helped him to keep the Scottish alliance with France strong and reliable. It was not endangered by the English weakness of the time, which also conduced to Border peace. And it was part of his plan for Scottish prosperity to promote trade links with Northern Europe.

At home the omens were far less fair. He at once set about

applying his father's policy of binding the crown to church, parliament and people, and was aided in that by the good and wise Bishop Kennedy, who had already done what he could to keep down the faction spirit during the minority. But his father's watchful suppression of aggressive nobles was a policy thrust on him as much as chosen. For Scotland held at his accession rather more than the seeds of civil war and in a young, handsome, arrogant Douglas a scarcely veiled threat to the king's power.

This James of the Fiery Face – one cheek was marred by a broad red birthmark – is reputed in history to have had a temperament rasher and more violent than his father's. Certainly his career is stained with one fiercely sudden deed that was nothing else than murder. But more than once in his short reign he showed, in spite of bitter provocation, an almost astonishing leniency.

His reign opened, after an English peace settlement, with a move that must have recalled the opening of his father's. James struck at the Livingstones, mis-handlers in chief of his minority, but there was only one execution, and there was a pardon that brought a good servant into the king's favour. James then turned to legislation, re-enacting some of his father's laws, including the re-establishment of the Court of Session and the codifying and clarifying of a legal tangle into a system. Matters were also put in train – signifying his enlightened acceptance of Bishop Kennedy's counsel – to give Scotland a second university and put Glasgow on something like level terms with St Andrews as a bishopric.

All this time the king had sought to win the threatening Douglas by friendliness and had indeed done him special honour with an embassy to Rome. But there came to light a Douglas alliance with enemies of the king in the north, and a piece of challenging Douglas high-handedness – the defiant execution of a prisoner whose release James had sought – brought the issue between king and noble to an unavoidable reckoning. It had a violent settlement, and it is mainly legend that provides the details, but it has to be remembered that James was dealing with a man who could raise perhaps half of armed Scotland against him and certainly wreck his work for the country's good. At any rate, story says that the king summoned the Douglas to Stirling, made a last vain effort to win loyalty, exposed the treachery of the secret alliance and had a request for its dissolution bluntly refused. The royal patience broke at that, forgot hospitality in a dagger thrust and set the example for Douglas's dispatch by those standing by. James was stricken with remorse, but the deed was done, and Scotland was soon in a blaze over the scotching of what was left of conspiracy.

It was a short sharp war, but with parliament, people and many of the barons on his side, James made a satisfactory end of it – and having done so, grew lenient. The Douglas inheriting the quarrel surrendered, was pardoned and was allowed to unite the family's southern lands again under one head. It proved a mistaken policy. Trouble was brewing in England – the Wars of the Roses were on the way – and this new Douglas earl sought some agreement with the Yorkist faction. That trespassed too far on the king's forgiveness. He took the field again, with stronger support than before, and at the end of the campaign the power of the house of Douglas was broken for good.

With the new domestic peace Scotland was able to take stock of itself, note its growing order and prosperity under a strong central government, look again at the beginnings of an impressive native architecture and see sufficient justification for the cheerful optimism of a parliament that met in 1458. Something of the temper of unitedness in the country is seen in the bustling preparations to man the Borders at the threat of renewed war with England. It came at last with the Yorkists' triumph over Henry of England and James's harbouring of the fugitive English queen. But with it came tragedy. James, leading an army into England, stopped to take Roxburgh, and there the bursting of a Scottish siege gun killed him. He was barely thirty, and again the heir was a boy, aged nine. But this time fate had less kindness for Scotland – the future king was of weaker stuff than his two predecessors.

The lad was crowned, within a week of his father's death, as James III, but it was to be nine years before he ruled alone. In this year of 1460, his mother, Mary of Gueldres, undertook the regency, and with the good Bishop Kennedy to advise her, the difficult opening months of the minority went well enough. But opposed factions were still striving for mastery in England, and Scottish intervention on one side brought trouble in the Highlands engineered by the other. Queen Mary wavered in her decision of policy and lost control of affairs. It was Kennedy who came to terms with the new English dynasty, and when he died in 1465 Scotland had reason to regret him. There was immediate intriguing for the guardianship of the young king, but – and the point is interesting – less harm came of it than usual. The truth seems to be that the strength of James II's government was real enough to survive his death, and although the young James was practically kidnapped by an enterprising noble there was no gross misuse of power by the new regent. Domestic legislation followed on sound enough lines, and it was in fact parliament, and not the regent, that authorized a marriage embassy to Scandinavia on the young king's behalf. It was a politic move, and it was successful. Scandinavian Princess Margaret brought to Scotland the strategic Orkney (as a dowry pledge), the settlement of an old dispute and an alliance with an apparently rising power in Europe. She and James were married in the summer of 1469, and the king, aged eighteen, set out to rule.

As usual, the first act of a reign following on a regency was the avenging of a wrong suffered in minority. James broke the Boyds, his youth's managers, and the affair had a sequel. His sister had married the head of the family, and when she was widowed she married again, with the king's approval, a Hamilton. And that marriage was the source of the Hamilton claim to the throne that was to disturb Scotland in the time of Mary Queen of Scots.

James's vengeance on the Boyds had in it something of the characteristic Stewart vigour, but in other ways he lacked the strong energy of his family. He had a taste for the arts and for learning, loved beauty and the splendour of fine show. But he was sensitive and retiring, easily overshadowed by his more forceful younger brothers, hesitant about responsibility, preferring study to action and inheriting perhaps an undue share of his family's strain of melancholy. With this gentler nature there went a quick affection, and where his affections were engaged James's heart was apt to rule his head and produce a odd blindness in judgment and a fatal leniency in punishment. In the ruggedness of the times he has an air of weakness. He was to pay dearly for the flaws in his character.

The opening years of the reign, however, were fair enough. There was some setting in order of internal affairs, although a scheme for a wise innovation in the church came to grief. The Scottish church lacked an archbishopric in its administrative system, and the lack had the disadvantage – usually in wartime – of prompting the nearest English archbishopric to

**114**

claim an irritating and inconvenient superiority. Kennedy's successor, Bishop Graham of Brechin, sought to remedy this, among other abuses, and succeeded with his statement of the Scottish case in Rome. But – the circumstances are obscure – he was under some sort of cloud in the king's favour, and he suffered for his effort at reform. A royal favourite secured his see and the new archiepiscopal title, Graham died in prison, and James lost a useful reformer of the church. This is curiously like some of the king's later misjudgments of men and affairs, of which too lightly dealt with treachery in his own family was the most disastrous instance. But meanwhile matters were in sufficiently good train for Scotland. Hovering war between England and Scotland was being kept at reasonable distance, more by the good sense of James's advisers than by his own. There was a prospect of marriage between his infant son and English Edward's daughter, and of a long truce to mark the alliance, and the king had used a moment of security and a mood of energy to break rebellious force in the Isles – although he spoilt the best effects of that by subsequent leniency. But in fact the real troubles of his reign were only about to begin, marking a black chapter in Stewart history.

James's younger brothers – Alexander, Duke of Albany, and John, Earl of Mar – were men now, and of a knightly mettle that made them, in the people's eyes, a striking contrast to the king. They were, perhaps, naturally jealous of the royal favourites, who seem to have been not wholly unworthy of contempt, and Albany, holding the wardenship of the Borders, had perhaps been flattered by overtures from England's Edward IV, no very scrupulous keeper of peace promises. There was an ugly rumour of conspiracy and the two princes were put in prison. The move was not popular, and a current of feeling began to run against the king. It was heightened when Albany effected a highly dramatic escape – his friends sent him a rope in a cask of wine – and worse than heightened when Mar died in somewhat mysterious circumstances. Between these happenings and James's increasing preference for his own clique of 'low-born' advisers over his nobles dissension and disunion in the country gathered weight. Meanwhile relations with England worsened. Edward, momentarily freed from preoccupation with France, showed small respect for his bargain with Scotland and James was provoked into deciding on war. The country was in no good case for it – uneasy, dissatisfied with the king's debasing of the coinage and in some discomfort from pestilence and a threat of famine. But there was mobilization in both countries, and there were some hostilities, although these did not extend much beyond a Border raid and a sea engagement that brought victory and reward to the Scottish seaman Sir Andrew Wood. For a moment there was a pause – in which it transpired that the duke of Albany, who had gone to France on his escape, was now in Edward's camp.

If treachery had been a rumour before, it was a fact now. James's brother was apparently ready to sacrifice Scotland in exchange for English help to the throne. He had agreed, as a would-be King of Scots, to bind himself to alliance with Edward, to break with France and to do homage for his kingdom once in possession of it. And with that astonishing secret treaty behind him he was marching on Berwick with the English army. James marched to meet the challenge, and the disgruntled nobles of Scotland took this opportunity to deal with the hated royal favourites, most of whom were accompanying the king to war. There was a famous meeting of men clothed in chain mail in Lauder Kirk in which the telling of the fable of the mice who agreed that the cat ought to wear a bell led to the leadership of the group by Archibald Douglas, fifth Earl of Angus, who in that moment had his name changed from Archibald the Grim to Archibald Bell-the-Cat for the rest of his days. The grim sequel to this was that the king's favourites (with one exception) died, each at the end of a rope over Lauder Bridge, and James found himself marching back to Edinburgh as his nobles' prisoner. The English, meeting no army to oppose them, captured Berwick and laid waste the surrounding country. But their advance on Edinburgh was barred. The nobles might have a quarrel with their king, but war was war.

And then things took an odd turn. Peace terms were negotiated, security was promised to Albany in return for reconciliation with James, and the English army turned back to finish their work in Berwick. Oddest of all, Albany rescued the king from Edinburgh Castle and was received into lavish royal favour. James's affection for his brother overruled all else. Albany was restored to his former titles and honours, collected an extra earldom and was actually made the King's Lieutenant of the Realm, with control of defence. Such excessive trust was bound, in view of all that had happened, to be betrayed afresh. In brief time Albany had renewed his secret parleys with Edward and was plotting for the throne. The plot was discovered, but still James was lenient. Albany lost the lieutenancy and his access to court but he was allowed to keep his lands and titles, even his Border wardenship. He promptly made fresh overtures to Edward, but his star was setting. The English king died, Albany was declared to have forfeited his life and possessions, and after one last desperate thrust, which was foiled, he escaped to France and was killed at a tourney there a year later. The whole episode displays persistent weakness in James.

**117**

Its end seemed at first to favour him. He had got rid of Albany without any danger to himself, and England, after some violent events about the throne, was settling under the rule of Henry Beaufort, who had plans for a peaceful realm and was well disposed towards Scotland. There was a new truce, subsequently extended, but James went back to an increasing desire for privacy and distaste for public affairs. It was an unwise policy. His son was growing up, a youth of brilliant promise, and disaffection soon set son against father. Almost in a moment, it seemed, there was a flare of civil war. The rebel lords chased the king across the Forth, secured the prince and declared him king in place of his father, whom they formally deposed. It is unlikely that the boy was more than a pawn in this game, but the game itself was seriously played. James raised the loyal north – he could be energetic when he was pressed – and might have had matters in his own hands had he been less eager to display his fatal leniency. There was a treaty that plainly could not last, another flare-up of struggle and the rebel and loyal forces met at Sauchieburn. It was a halfhearted sort of fight, and the king was quickly out of it, on a bolting horse. Tragedy followed swift on that headlong gallop. James was thrown as he rode, carried into a cottage by kindly mill folk, and found there by a mounted stranger who rode up to hear a woman cry for a priest for the king. This man – his identity has never been certainly established – declared that he was a priest and was led by an innocent guide to where the king lay. And James III was shrived – with a dagger.

The new king was only fifteen. Yet for once a minority brought little evil in its train, and under the brilliance of James IV Scotland seemed to be entering what promised to be another and more glorious Golden Age. Actually, Stewart splendour was to touch only a brief peak; what fate had in store for king and people was disaster.

The omens of the reign that opened in 1488 were at first fair enough – the chief of them the personality of James himself. He soon became a prominent figure in his people's lives and minds. Even granting that the men who came into power during his teens were less greedy and more just than those some other minorities had known, it is still significant that James's advent to full kingship came about without crisis of any kind. He grew gradually, imperceptibly, inevitably into active rule. It was as if the man became king while Scotland was still wondering at the boy.

James IV shared with his great-grandfather the best of the Stewart aptitude for kingship. He saw Scotland as a whole and tried to rule it as such, and because he saw this unity as something to be maintained in the best interests of his people, he brought to the business of ruling a tremendous sense of responsibility. And the field in which he had to exercise it was bigger than any known to his predecessors. For Scotland in James's time was reaching the zenith of that movement that made her a European power. At the end of the fifteenth century, medieval Europe was giving place to the Renaissance Europe that was dominated by the interplay of three great nations – Spain, France and England. Scotland, traditionally the enemy of England and the ally of France, could not but be drawn into international affairs, and it fell to James to hold the balance between the rivalries and intrigues of the European contenders. No other King of Scots, of any era, was so entreated for support by foreign embassies. The ambition or rashness of a lesser man might have succumbed disastrously to such pride-nourishing appeals. But James, the responsible ruler constant for peace, held a difficult and precarious bal-

**119**

ance of power until not misjudgment or folly but the sheer pressure of events forced his hand.

Such influence in international affairs could have been wielded only by a king who was master of a united kingdom. And James was that – not so much by force of arms as by force of personality. He had good looks, charm and strong physical energy – attributes that, along with his accessibility, open-handedness and keen sense of justice, endeared him to a people who have always warmed to their rulers as men rather than kings. He won the church with his real reverence for religion and his scholar's interest in things scholarly. He fostered education, added another university (Aberdeen) to the country's existing two, took a practical interest in the new invention of printing and brought the arts to his court. And his drive, his obvious fitness for leadership, and perhaps especially his genuineness for Scotland, broke down the old opposition of nobles to the crown. It was this man of strength and charm who finally won the Highlands, won them so completely that when a change from conciliation to a less friendly policy threatened disturbance it needed only the renewal of the king's trust to strengthen the weakened bonds. It was to James IV that later Stewarts owed the persistent devotion of the northwest.

The background for all this was an increasingly prosperous Scotland. Scottish trade required chiefly peace in order to flourish, and in the early years of James's reign, helped by the king's interest in the founding of something like Scottish sea power, it grew rapidly. The quickening of national life, which was expressed in brisker commerce, the spread of learning, the development of the arts and the activity of marked intellectual vigour – it was the age of Dunbar and Gavin Douglas – was reflected also in the life of the people. Scotland's folk

**120**

lived well, in the matter of clothes and food, and foreign envoys frequently reported to their masters on the country's sound condition. But there has come down to us from this vivid, eager time an odd hint of contemporary feverishness in living. James's court, vital, splendid, had a share of it. It comes out often in Dunbar's poetry, a curiously fey undercurrent caught forever in that haunting refrain of his *Timor mortis conturbat me*. There are signs of it in James himself, in the streak of dark morbidity that marked his religion, in those swift transitions from lively relish of the pride of life to grim penance. It is, perhaps, too easy to read romantic tragedy into the events of his life – from that killing of his father, which is said to have always haunted his conscience, through the restless love affairs that brought him at last the heartbreak of beautiful Margaret Drummond's death, to the crushing disaster that finally befell him at Flodden. But if the shadow of Flodden seems to overlie his whole reign, it is not, somehow, only in our preknowledge of that catastrophe.

For the moment, however, that belonged to the unknown future. In the immediate present of the last years of the fifteenth century, all was promise for Scotland. There was prompt action to set the recently disturbed affairs of the kingdom in order and a hint of the prestige to come. James was only just crowned when a Spanish embassy arrived in Linlithgow with some talk of a marriage. A year later there was a brief reappearance of the civil war, but it was firmly and wisely put down, not to raise its head again until the end of the reign. Skirmishes with English privateers were rather more serious, in view of the expanding overseas trade, but Scotland still had Sir Andrew Wood, and that redoubtable seaman was more than a match for his opponents. James, aided by the wise counsel of Bishop Elphinstone of Aber-

121

deen, in the Kennedy tradition of bishop-statesmen, settled to his growth into kingship, and parliaments were busy with domestic legislation. England offered a truce and a marriage. Scotland refused the marriage but took the truce – a six years' one, it was – and James, now twenty, set about his peaceful and personal conquest of the Highlands. Aberdeen got its university, Edinburgh its College of Surgeons.

Then in 1495 James took a hand in an odd ploy. The affair was English, a revival of the old York-Lancaster quarrel, with the Yorkists putting up Perkin Warbeck as the lawful king of England. It is difficult to justify the Scots king's intervention in this business, but he could not then know that Warbeck was another pretender, a second Lambert Simnel. He had no quarrel with England, although he had no reason to think well of Henry VII, and in the beginning at least he may have simply befriended a young prince kept by force from his heritage. There may have been a touch of shrewdness about it too. At any rate, he gave hospitality to the claimant, and there were interesting sequels. Henry hastened to offer marriage with his daughter Margaret, aged six. The English king's alarm was doubtless responsible for the arrival of another Spanish embassy, offering an alternative marriage to the English one, which James had refused. And France, momentarily not anxious for a war between Scotland and England, dispatched an embassy of mediation. The King of Scots was being pressed, and in addition to this multiplying of embassies there was some underground work going on as well. Perhaps out of resentment, much out of honour and a little out of policy, James declared war, and there was a raid over the Border, with defeat of a counter-raid. But the affair fizzled out. Warbeck wavered, thought to cut his Scottish venture and try again in the south of England, and was there captured and hanged. Neither James nor Henry really wanted war, and by 1497 there was truce, negotiated by an envoy of Spain.

Henry VII subsequently renewed his importunities for a marriage. But James was twenty-six, the proposed English bride was a child of ten, and there was his mistress Margaret Drummond, who of all the women placed by fact and legend in the king's life seems alone to have had his heart. Romanticists lament that he did not marry this Margaret. Historians are not so sure. It seems certain that James thought of it and hesitated. Then there came the sinister and tragic death by poisoning of Margaret Drummond and her two sisters and an end to James's indifference to the English marriage proposal.

In 1503 Margaret Tudor was married with great splendour at Holyrood, and the King of Scots, a troubled man with dark and dangerous years to face, had a petulant child for queen. History has not been over-kind to this Queen Margaret. She was never able to see Scotland as her husband saw it, a noble ideal for which to make sacrifices. She never shared his vision of a peaceful prosperity, but she was only fifteen when she became a queen, and the years of her growing up must have been difficult. The continual contrast between a great position and the lack of stature to occupy it might well have daunted a stronger character than hers. And it was a great position. In the years after his marriage, James was acting often in the role of peacemaker in foreign disputes, and his court was a busy place of great affairs and the comings and goings of embassies. Scotland, thriving at home under the domestic activities of king and parliament, was wielding the influence of a major power abroad. Few countries seemed readier to ripen and bear notable fruit in the warmth of the promised Renaissance. But English victory at the Battle of Flodden in 1513 intervened.

**123**

James has been blamed for that disaster. He had invaded England – a piece of unnecessary folly, it was said, war-making in an outmoded tournament spirit of war-making for war-making's sake, at best a quixotically chivalrous sally that was bound to fail since small Scotland was no match for mighty England. But war with England was not so much a matter of choice as something inevitable, for England, strong in unity again after the civil war, and determinedly governed, was almost bound to try conclusions with her old enemy. Nor was James a war-maker. The motive in all his actions had been peace. He had worked hard and paid dear for it at home and abroad, and when he went to war he went reluctantly, as one who saw his life's work endangered thereby, forced into it by threats to his country's independence and by the peril of his French ally. On any basis except one that denies Scotland the right to pursue her own foreign policy, the move to war was justified. It was, moreover, strategically timed, and if not adequately equipped for success – the English army seems to have been superior in arms with the new longbow – carried out with a force in which its leader could put ample trust.

Flodden was a disaster of inferior generalship and an apparently unwise use of tactics more European than Scottish. But its magnitude was far beyond that of a crushing military defeat that killed a king and took a fearful toll of lords and commons on the field of battle. Flodden swept away at one blow the splendid edifice of power that James had built up for Scotland. His son was a baby, and his queen, left widowed and without his shaping influence, developed the Tudor characteristics of selfishness and avarice that her brother, Henry VIII, was to make notorious in history. The kingdom and the country slid from the crest of the wave deep into the trough.

The depths were apparent almost at once in that mourning

**124**

winter of 1513. Flodden had mowed a great swathe through the order of the generations. There was much the same sort of gap between youth and age that our times knew at the end of the First World War. The nation's choice of leaders lay largely between old men and boys. The dead king had decreed that his queen should be regent, acting with a council, so long as she remained unmarried. In practice that tended to mean the rule of Margaret and the Earl of Angus, head of the self-seeking Red Douglas house that had consistently put Scottish interests second to its own.

By all the omens, Scotland was in for a difficult minority, and parliament, perhaps the staunchest inheritor of James's policy and purpose, was uneasy. It spoke for the mass of the people, and the people, along with the church and some of the nobles, were strong for the old French alliance. But the queen was an English princess, and she had the backing of other nobles, headed by Angus, who were not unappreciative of English money. In no time the country was distracted by hostile factions. Then the queen married Angus. There was a brief tussle to prevent her retention of ruling power and ample legal justification for a change of regents. The new one was James's cousin, the Duke of Albany, who came from France, where he had been born and bred. He was practically a Frenchman and seemed certain to ensure the continuance of the old Franco-Scottish alliance as a makeweight against English aggression. But his difficulties were well nigh insuperable. He had to hold the power of government not only against Angus and the queen and their party but also against the sometimes open, sometimes underground, but persistent intervention of Henry VIII. He held it for nine years, against opposition that was a tangled tissue of intrigue and treachery, flickers of war, plots to capture the boy prince. Then he went

**125**

down in a gallant but desperate effort to meet the English challenge by force of arms.

There followed a most unedifying struggle between the queen and her Douglas husband for possession of the king and the power that went with his wardship. The boy swung from hand to hand in a sickening captivity that he came to hate as he came to hate his captors. In his last years as the prisoner of Angus, who had finally worsted the queen in this duel, the young James was privy to two attempts at armed rescue. They failed, but a chance of escape came his way in 1528, and the boy – he was only sixteen, but old, not surprisingly, for his years – seized it. There was a careless Douglas guard over him in his prison at Falkland. He found the means to win one or two of their servants, and one dawn saw him riding for Stirling in the guise of a groom. There was discovery and vain pursuit, but James was free. And Angus sought safety in his strongest castle. He had something to fear from a King of Scots who had known Douglas wardship. It came, quickly enough. Angus was cited for treason, refused to appear, was forfeited of life and possessions, and was finally driven from Scotland, in a brisk little war between a new crown and an old regent that set the traditional stamp of blood-letting on the end of a minority.

This fifth James in the rule of Scotland had his share of the Stewart characteristics. He had charm, he was personally well favoured, and he valued scholarship and the arts, although his restless childhood had interrupted his training in them. He was Stewart enough to lay hold of the traditional policy of his house, at home and abroad, and he had the kingly dignity that neither interfered with nor suffered from his readiness to meet any of his people who sought him. Scotland called him 'the King of the Commons' for that. He was strong for the weak against the oppressor. Profligate he may have been, but that one looseness in an otherwise disciplined life was the fruit of Angus's teaching – a different childhood might well have made a different man.

His worst flaw went far deeper – he could not endure. Long odds he could face and fight – once – but failure defeated him, betrayal broke his heart. And in his Scotland, with English money ready to feed the rebellious arrogance of the nobles, and a church still patriotic but moving through corruption to collapse, there were few whom he could trust. It was an odd turn of fate that gave to Scotland, at the beginning of that bribed treachery that was to weaken her government until the death of England's Elizabeth, a king who could not cope with it.

What he could cope with, at the start of his reign, he dealt with faithfully enough – the flicker of rebellion and private war among his nobles that followed the disappearance of Angus. He quelled the Borders, made a truce (and preparations for dealing with its breach) with Henry in the south, saw to a revolt in the far north, and brought his father's policy of appeasement and his own personal charm to the reconquest of the Isles. Lawlessness he put down firmly, and he added notably to the machinery for doing so with the College of Justice. Foreign affairs gave more trouble. Henry had a modern flair for making war under cover of a paper peace and kept the Borders uneasy. By way of maintaining a balance of power, James was inclined to the traditional French alliance and had thoughts of a French queen. But the French king was reluctant to provoke Henry. From foreign sources, too, came something new to trouble politics – the challenge of Calvinism to the traditional church. Its first repercussions in Scotland took James unwillingly away from the Stewart tolerance

**127**

he would have preferred. He had to meet his churchmen's demand for stronger measures against the new doctrines. It was a significant straw in the wind, the beginning of a fresh foothold within Scotland for the newly Protestant Henry outside. And things began to drift towards the inevitable breach between the two countries.

Its arrival was helped by James's French marriages. In fact there were two. James's first bride, Madeleine, the French king's daughter, was only for months a figure in Scots history. He married her in Paris in January of 1537. She came to Scotland in May and died, of consumption, in July. She was perhaps seventeen. And James, the Stewart succession in danger, had to have a queen. One was found, again in France. She was the lovely Mary of Guise, a woman of spirit and courage. James carried her off from none other than his uncle, Henry, who was then paying one of his periodic visits to the marriage market, and it is quite possible that Henry never forgave either Scotland or France for the hurt to his vanity.

James and Mary were married at St Andrews in 1538, and an already brilliant court took on added brilliance with a queen to honour and entertain. For a while Scotland glowed with the rich splendour and the heady vigour of living that had been known before Flodden. But the shadow of coming war lay over these colours, and perhaps no one was deceived.

Trouble was indeed mounting too quickly and too steadily to be ignored. The religious difficulty was allying itself with the English one. James needed the support of his church and had to support its attacks on heresy. He had also to try to reform some of its more obvious abuses. Both processes made enemies as well as friends for him. The nobles who resented his firm hand were ready enough to follow Henry, who was showing by example what wealth could be squeezed from an

**128**

old faith in the name of a new and was, moreover, exhorting James and the Scots to use Protestantism to the same advantage. War continued to come nearer. Late in 1541 Henry had travelled north to an apparently arranged conference that James had not attended and was angry enough in consequence to raise the old claim of overlordship. Promptly the Border country was swept by raids and counter-raids. Early in 1542 Ireland did not help matters with the offer to James of a crown that Henry had demanded. James refused, but Henry's urge to war had a new impetus. There was an official invasion, which was repulsed, but peace was at an end and James had to take the initiative. He had neither leaders to trust nor an army that was united. His first force he had to disband while the English troops it might have pursued escaped over the Border. His second he was leading himself into England when he became ill. He gave its leadership to the wrong man of two who claimed the right; in enemy country they quarrelled over it, and the army that should have been solid split into factions. A well-trained English force, smaller than the Scots but with a general who knew an opportunity when he saw one, drove disorder into the Scottish ranks. There could be only one result – defeat, panic, slaughter.

That was the rout of Solway Moss, in late November 1542, and the news of its shame, as much as his illness, killed the king before the year was out. There was one last twist of the knife in his wound. Two sons borne to him by Mary of Guise had died in infancy. He learned now, as he lay sick at Falkland, that his queen was delivered of a daughter. And, runs the contemporary chronicle, 'he spake little from then forth, but turned his back to his lords and his face to the wall,' a dying man who knew in his death the probable end of rule and royalty in the male line of his house.

**129**

# CHAPTER XI

# THE TRAGIC QUEEN

It is important to see clearly, as background for the tragic reign that was now to play out its fateful scenes, what manner of Scotland this was in which the sovereign was a girl child not a week old and her guardian a young queen dowager. It was a Scotland in an even more dangerous condition than at the beginning of James V's reign. For it was, or was about to be, the Scotland of the Reformation. And what is often misunderstood about that event is its double significance. The story of the Reformation is the story of a revolution, not only religious (and to some extent, inevitably social) but political as well.

The heart of it, of course, was religious conviction – of a kind that, at its peak of intensity and sincerity, made men ready to slay or be slain for their beliefs, counting nothing a makeweight in the scales against their idea of the divine purpose. At first, men of that calibre were few. It was much more mundane things, like the mounting ambition and greed of some Scottish nobles, and the aggressive opportunism of England, that really nourished the first growths of the Reformation, but it took its real and ruling character from the fervour of the few, as that spread gradually to the many. Nothing less could have driven Scotland to the violence of the Protestant break with the Catholic past or so quickly imperilled the independence of the kingdom and its people's firm sense of nationality. These were to stand fast yet a little longer, with the memory of Wallace, Bruce and Bannockburn – that trinity of patriotism – as sustaining power against the first shock of the ecclesiastical challenge. The peril, and the shock, came from that political force that marched with the religious in the new movement. Already, in the time of James V, it had helped an English king to a novel foothold against a King of Scots within Scotland itself. Now there was to develop a split in the organization of the kingdom that helped ultimately to undermine its separate integrity.

Hitherto the heart of the state and the builders of its power had been its kings. Scotland's kings had worked, when they were good kings, for unity and the rule of law and order, defending these against both the anarchistic ambition of nobles and the attacks of outside enemies. But they had only succeeded in doing so with the aid of the church and of the people. Now these two traditional allies of the crown were leaving it. The Reformation, religious movement although it always was at the core, first broke in Scotland as an anti-national movement. It is easy to see how that happened. The Roman Catholic Church, even in corruption, was strong for the crown, for Scottish independence and for the old French alliance against England. In theory, reforming Protestantism ought to have been able to distinguish a creed from a political philosophy and to confine its onslaught to what it really had a quarrel with – the old faith. But, in fact, creed and philosophy were nearly indistinguishable in practice. And the attack of the new religion had the backing of England and of certain Scots nobles, for both of whom it was a convenient stalking horse. England was hot for a Protestant Scotland – because it would be a Scotland separated from still Catholic France, weakened by internal division and thus ripe for English conquest. And what the nobles saw, and were ready to use the English backing to get, was loot in the destruction of the old church, with licence for themselves in the decay of crown power.

There was ample reason in all that – political necessity and the strategy of defence, to say nothing of personal preference – to keep the crown Catholic while the Reformation was getting a grip of the country. And in an age before tolerance was possible that meant more or less serious division. But it went even deeper. Even when Protestantism had taken hold of the country, friendliness was more than the crown could, in the nature of things, give to the new faith. That was because the leaders of the Calvinism that ultimately fastened on Scotland could not admit, in any rivalry to their fervent allegiance to their conception of divine truth, any other allegiance either to crown or country. Their loyalty was to God, in the new revelation, and other loyalties were as nothing beside it. It was magnificent, but it was appallingly dangerous. It could, and did, let down Scotland's defences to the invader. While the crown stood outside the kirk it gave unscrupulous nobles every chance to dress up treason as God's work, and it encouraged the growth of a new national consciousness that gave no place to that institution of kingship on which strong and independent government in Scotland had been built. Kirk and crown were thus to be locked in a struggle to govern. With the aid of England, the kirk won – for a time, and when that time was over Scotland had no crown of its own left.

It was to the stage that was being set for that devastating struggle that there came, first, a young queen dowager and then, eighteen years afterwards, a girl in her teens, equipped

**132**

for a crucial task with little else than the danger of her own youthful charm.

Mary of Guise, inheriting her dead husband's problem, was spiritedly and courageously loyal to his thwarted effort to handle it. To aid her she had, of course, France – across the sea – and at home Cardinal Beaton of St Andrews, a man not faultless by any means but of able strength in defence of his church, of Scottish independence and of the crown. He was almost the only Scot of eminence whom she could trust, and he happened to be the man who was readiest to defy Henry VIII. The English king seemed to have Scotland within his grasp after Solway Moss. He had bribed the freed prisoners of the rout to act as his agents in Scotland. The Earl of Arran, one of the regents and heir presumptive to the throne, was his man, and plans were afoot to kidnap queen and cardinal. Most of this proceeded under cover of a peaceful move – an offer of treaty between the two countries sealed by a marriage contract between Henry's son and Mary's daughter. Henry's intrigues were a little too transparent, however. He was offering to make Arran King of Scotland north of Forth as his vassal, and Scottish opinion began to harden against the treaty and the marriage. By 1544 there was war, ravaging the eastern Lowlands. It blazed, in cruel spasms, throughout 1545. Cardinal Beaton was murdered, but Mary of Guise kept up the fight. She was helped first by the arrival of French troops and treasure, then by the death of Henry, who was succeeded by a minor, and finally by the appearance of another bridegroom for her daughter, the young Dauphin, heir to France. The match was made. The future Queen of Scots, who had been sent for safety to the Priory of Inchmahome, in the Lake of Menteith, sailed from Dumbarton to be educated at the French court. She was then in her sixth year.

**133**

Her mother turned to hold her difficult regency. Outside Scotland, fortune favoured her courage. Division in England relaxed the war. In 1553 the feeble boy who was the English King died, to be succeeded by his half-sister Mary, a devout Catholic, and in 1558 the Franco-Scottish marriage was safely solemnized to make a link between the two countries that duly impressed Europe. But at home Mary of Guise was less fortunate. For lack of Scots about her to trust, she relied on French advisers, and it cost her her popularity. The religious conflict dividing the country had not yet steadied from spasmodic outbursts to a sustained drive, but the old church was continually weakening and was seeking help from the crown rather than lending it strength. John Knox had appeared to whip up Calvinistic fervour and be a lance in rest for the manoeuvring nobles.

Things moved towards a crisis, and Mary had worn herself out trying to avert it. England's Catholic queen died, to be succeeded by the Protestant Elizabeth. That was a blow, not wholly softened by later news from France, where an accident during a tournament had killed King Henri and as suddenly made the Dauphin and his Scots bride king and queen of France. For Elizabeth's accession meant that English money and promise of arms reappeared behind Scottish Protestantism, and very quickly there was religious civil war (with mercenaries on both sides) north of the Border. In the middle of it Mary of Guise died, trying for a settlement of tolerance until the last. The year was 1560.

For ruler Scotland now had the queen of France, but she was in France. In Scotland the Protestant nobles and the kirk had swept into power when Mary of Guise went down. They had, as it happened, a full year in which to work their will. For although the queen of France was widowed a few months after her mother's death, she did not come to Scotland to rule as Mary Queen of Scots until 1561. And by that time the triumphant nobles and kirk had consolidated their power – the Reformation was an established fact that the country, by and large, was coming to accept.

Mary's position was from the outset one of enormous difficulty. Like many another Stewart before her, succeeding to the throne after a minority, she had to cope with treacherously ambitious nobles, weakened crown power and the enmity of England. To these political difficulties were added for her acute religious ones; indeed the two were inextricably intertwined. She was the Catholic queen of a country mainly and militantly Protestant. If she sought to restore her faith, as she might well have been tempted to do with the support that seemed to await such a move, she would plunge the country into civil war and embroil it with England. To turn Protestant was impossible for one of her upbringing and antecedents.

No monarch since the time of the second Robert had had to face such a tangle of problems as now faced Mary. She brought to them three traditional Stewart gifts – courage, charm and quick intelligence. But she had neither the years nor the training for statecraft, while she did have her share of the Stewart failings of misjudging character and misplacing trust. She had no army, no great wealth, no well-organized and powerful group of crown supporters and no reliable foreign ally.

It was the traditional Stewart policy she set herself to follow – an independent and united Scotland, held in a framework of law and order maintained by the central strength of the crown, speaking and acting especially for the inarticulate commons. She followed it gallantly, in spite of insults to herself and her faith, working quietly with the best of the Protestant lords for what was deemed Scotland's good, winning youth and gaiety to her court in response to her own, earning the beginnings of affection from the people with her spirited grace and courage.

Proof of her quality came quickly. There was an Ogilvie-Gordon dispute in Edinburgh, and a younger son of the Earl of Huntly, who was the head of the Gordons and the chief Catholic noble, landed in prison. Mary was on a royal progress in the north, and the indignant Huntly in Inverness showed his resentment. Now Huntly had been nearly as deep in treason, as much a troubler of the peace, as greedy a hand with church loot as the worst of the Protestant lords. If, at this juncture, he thought he could safely provoke disorder because he professed the same faith as the queen, he learned his error. Mary struck without hesitation, eager Protestant lords lending weight to the blow. Huntly was killed in battle, a son was executed and the revolt quelled. The thing was a lesson to all factions – the crown had shown an unlooked-for strength, and the country profited, moving steadily in the direction of unity under tolerance, impressed by the influence and evidence of the forces of stabilization.

But progress could not continue so simply. The stronger and more harmonious Scotland became, the more English fears mounted. And there was the matter of the queen's marriage. Suitors swarmed. It was at this moment that Darnley appeared. Henry Lord Darnley was a person of considerable importance in both kingdoms. He was next heir after Mary and his own (Catholic) mother to the throne of England, and he was next heir after the Hamiltons (the century-old marriage of James III's sister was vital now) and his own father to the throne of Scotland. If Mary married him, she obviously

**136**

strengthened her English claim and at the same time fore-
stalled possible trouble with a Scottish Pretender. Moreover,
Darnley was young and personable. The flaw in Darnley's at-
tractions, as events were to show, was his character, and Elizabeth, who could read men, has been credited with a deliberate attempt to lure Mary into marriage with a scoundrel
whose failure as king might well be her ruin as queen. The
thing is possible, and in so far as it is possible, it would have
been open to James, Earl of Moray, who could read men as
aptly as Elizabeth and as aptly assess their usefulness as pawns.
But between Mary and Moray, an illegitimate son of James V
and therefore her half-brother, there was deepening estrange-
ment. She doubted, not without reason, his trustworthiness,
and when Darnley came to Scotland all the omens for the
match seemed fair. It was made, with all the official approval
that Mary could conveniently recognize, and in 1565 she and
Darnley were married.

Almost at once there was trouble. Since Darnley was
Catholic, so far as he was anything, the marriage roused religious anger. In 1565 the Protestant lords seized the chance to
rebel, with Moray and the promise of English backing. But
there was no popular enthusiasm for the revolt, and Mary
drove the rebels over the Border in what came to be known
as the Chaseabout Raid. It was the peak of her success. She
had twice nipped civil war in the bud, had broken the most
dangerously treacherous nobles, was gaining ground in the
move for religious tolerance and had strengthened her crown
not only in Scotland but in its claim to the English succession.

These things might have been the herald of still greater
successes if the man she had married had possessed ordinary
intelligence and average decency. But Darnley was a fool, a

**137**

vain, vicious, treacherous fool, so stupidly selfish that self-interest could not teach him what he failed to learn of loyalty. He was marked out to be the tool of greater men, and within a few months the queen's enemies had worked him into a raging jealousy over David Rizzio, Mary's Italian secretary and protégé. There was a particularly ugly plot, with its chief aim and purpose the death of the queen and of the child she was about to bear, the treachery of the rebel lords cruelly cloaked by Darnley in the role of wronged husband striking Rizzio down.

Everyone knows how near it came to success, how armed men entered Holyrood one March night in 1566, won access by a private stair to the little room where the queen was at supper with her friends, and there slew Rizzio before her eyes, her husband standing with her enemies. Darnley was frightened – his wife thought him insanely jealous, but he knew himself the instrument of a conspiracy that threatened to miscarry – and in that spasm of fear Mary won him over, within a day made a chance of escape and by night was riding for safety with Darnley to Dunbar, in the hold of the Earl of Bothwell, one of the few nobles whom she still trusted. The plot failed, but Mary was in no state to take advantage of its defeat. There had to be pardons for the Rizzio crime and a smoothing over of deep-rooted trouble. Mary's son was born.

Scottish history for the next few months leaps into a wild nightmare of unproved and unprovable possibilities, suspicions, fantasies, a world of tortuous and baffling shadows lit only here and there by the certainty of a few facts. The worst construction that has been put upon the tangle of events is that Mary, in love with Bothwell, plotted with him the murder of Darnley, married her lover and went down in just expiation of great guilt. There is no proof. The best construc-

tion is that Darnley was murdered by the men he had betrayed, Bothwell having no direct hand in it, that suspicion of
guilt was directed against the queen for a set purpose, that she
turned to Bothwell out of need for his strength for Scotland
as much as out of liking and that she went down because that
alliance was too formidable for her enemies to allow it to
grow in power. Again, there is no proof. It is not even possible to compromise and say with any certainty that the probable truth lies here, or there, between those two extremes.

The few certain facts are these. In January 1567 Darnley
was seriously ill near Glasgow. The queen made an effort at
reconciliation that came to nothing.

At the end of January Darnley arrived in Edinburgh, lodg-
ing at a house outside the town, known as Kirk o' Field.
Early in February the house went up in an explosion.
Darnley's body, when found in the garden of the house, was
clad in a shirt and bore the marks not of gunpowder but of
strangulation. The first results were indignation, rumour, ugly
scandal and a swing of popular sympathy away from the
queen. Early in April Bothwell appeared for trial, with a tail
of armed men, and was acquitted. Shortly afterwards, certain
men (uncertain, really, since they are shadowy) signed a
document supporting him in a plan to marry the queen. In
May the marriage took place according to the Protestant
form, Bothwell having put through a hasty divorce.
(Whether Mary was forced into it or went into it willingly, is
unknown. There is much to suggest coercion.) There was
then a curiously uneasy pause while both sides gathered armies, armies whose knights and nobles, on both sides, suggest
that control in Scotland, and not the avenging or defence of
guilt, was the real issue to be fought out. Mary and Bothwell
met the opposing lords at Carberry Hill. There was hardly a

**139**

battle. Flight was made possible for some of the queen's supporters. Bothwell took a chance to escape. Mary surrendered on terms and went to imprisonment on the island of Loch Leven.

It was the beginning of the end. What really helped to seal her doom was that she had an heir, a boy prince who could take her place in the succession yet be helplessly forced, more easily than she could be forced, to lend the seal of authority to factions eager to plunder the realm. The young James was, in fact, used against her in pawn fashion before she left Scotland. Meanwhile, she was threatened with trial, although none of the evidence that was said to be so damning to her cause was then produced. Instead she had to abdicate and name Moray as regent.

There was small help at home and none abroad. Moray promptly crushed her pitiful little army at Langside. Desperate, she turned to Elizabeth, who was apparently overjoyed at her escape and profuse in promises of help. Mary rode south, spent her last night in Scotland at Dundrennan Abbey, and the next day crossed Solway – to another prison.

Even so, the end was not yet. Elizabeth's promises resolved themselves into arbitration at an official investigation. It was throughout nigh farcical. Mary was not heard in person. She was kept at the other end of England while the commissioners for her defence argued in London. The notorious Casket Letters, which were alleged to cover her with guilt in a conspiracy with Bothwell to murder Darnley, appeared briefly as originals but chiefly as translations. They were never shown to Mary and apparently did not impress the court. Its verdict was the equivalent of 'not proven', which the Regent Moray shrewdly interpreted as meaning that Elizabeth had no serious complaint against what had been done and would support his rule in Scotland. Mary was in effect sentenced to life imprisonment.

Her cause provoked flickers of civil war in England and Scotland, with raids and counter-raids over the Border. Moray, the one man who could have worked for the stability of Scotland despite the dangers of this time, fell to a pistol shot in a feud, and the two regencies that succeeded his were short-lived. Their weakness helped to raise the hopes of Mary's supporters in Scotland, for her cause at this time seemed likely to win foreign intervention. But it came to nothing, and in 1572 the Regent Morton, strong where the two previous regents had been weak, extinguished the last embers of the war on Mary's behalf, and her last chance, although she struggled on, was extinguished with them.

For the rest of her life Mary was a prisoner of Elizabeth, and the place of her imprisonment was frequently changed, her final prison being Fotheringhay Castle in Northamptonshire. During this time there was a series of allegations that she was involved in pro-Catholic plots to depose Elizabeth. She was at last accused of being implicated in a plot by Anthony Babington against Elizabeth's life, and having been tried by a court of Elizabeth's appointing was, in late 1586, condemned to be executed. There was a long delay before Elizabeth signed the warrant, but her hand was at last forced, and this was done in February the following year. Mary received the news with great serenity and was beheaded a week later.

# CHAPTER XII

# *T*HE UNION OF THE CROWNS

In Scotland, after Mary's forced abdication, there was constant friction between factions, some wrath in the new church over attempts by the civil power to manipulate the kirk for its own ends and much jockeying for possession of the young James. But these things changed in 1583, when he escaped from wardship and in typical Stewart fashion announced his determination to rule. He was just seventeen.

Typical Stewart, however, he himself was not. Physically he had neither strength nor good looks, defects that helped him to that lack of personal presence that was always to be noticed about his kingship. He was timid, too, for much the same reasons, with, as additional factors, his troubled childhood and frequent fear for his life during youth. From his mother, on the other hand, he drew his intelligence, and it was a good one, not merely scholarly, although it was that, but also shrewd in practical matters, and upheld by an odd, nervous sort of resolution that could tremble but somehow not falter of its purpose. He was, in fact, politician and not man of action.

He came to the throne of a virtually new country that the old Stewart tradition had already, in his mother, failed to rule. The chief force in it was the Kirk. It was a Kirk that lacked wealth, but it was rich in exalted independence, in fervour, and therefore — as it gathered the Lowlands behind it — in power. And it was settling into a form that, for two reasons, challenged the rule of any civil government. For one thing, its democratic form — the people made themselves heard in the supreme General Assembly through the chain of elected kirk sessions and presbyteries — was bound up by religious fervour with the ordinary business of living as no government could be. And for another, the Kirk as a divine institution knew only divine principles and knew these as absolute.

For the backing of that government in this struggle James VI had practically nothing, except the half-mystic, half-legal power of the crown. Money he had none. Currency values were falling; the cost of government was increasing (the era of the professional army, for instance, had begun); the wealth of the old Church had fallen to the plundering nobles. It was only on a pension from Elizabeth, more readily promised than paid, that James was able to finance himself; and the fact kept him in a continual twist of shifty device and crafty cunning in order to hold his place against challenging Kirk, aggressive nobles and English intrigue — while he waited for Elizabeth to die. Peaceful accession to the English throne was his only hope.

James's first move was to approach Elizabeth, now fifty, for a definite settlement of the succession, and when she refused, obviously to gauge the mettle of this newcomer, James seemed quick to show her. He sounded Catholic opinion abroad and made overtures to what was left of his mother's Catholic support at home. In the spring of 1584, with the help of the Earl of Arran, on whom he leant heavily at this time, James struck at another attempt to kidnap him, and there was a beheading and some forfeitures. Elizabeth momentarily took alarm.

**143**

There came a moment in the movement of foreign affairs when it was convenient for Elizabeth to secure James on her side of the European balance of power. There was a treaty, and a more or less implicit acceptance of the Scottish king as the English heir. There was also, in quick sequence, English backing for a Scottish intrigue against him, and the implication of his mother in a Catholic plot against Elizabeth. James was captured by a group of his nobles, and while he was thus held, Mary was formally indicted for treason. There was a curious surge of feeling in Scotland at the prospect of her death on an English scaffold, but it could not move far towards saving her – and James did little to help it. He made it sufficiently clear that in the alternative of his mother's death and his prospective title he had only one choice. That was enough, and in due course Mary was executed.

James married Anne of Denmark and found himself lectured by the Church over her too Popish anointing at the coronation. He was in fact in danger from the nobles and the Kirk. In 1591 would-be abductors had fire and sword at his chamber door in Holyrood before the attempt was driven off, and in 1592 a General Assembly demanded and got for a minority of extremists a 'liberty' that in fact brought the Kirk's challenge to the crown boldly into the open. Fiery Andrew Melville, minister of the word and fanatic leader of the extremists, told him to his face that he was no more than 'God's sillie vassal'. James had seen the business of government go from his hands to the Kirk's and had later been driven by threatening bankruptcy to delegate some of his remaining powers to a sort of financial cabinet – a committee of eight known as the Octavians.

The tide then began to turn, helped by the discovery that the king's reforming 'Octavians' were harder to thole than the

King himself and by James's own astute move from Edinburgh to Linlithgow. The capital took fright. The religious riot collapsed, its leaders discredited, and when king and court came back they met an enthusiastic welcome.

And it came at last, the thing that he had so patiently and so carefully waited and prepared for. In March 1603, Elizabeth died. The news reached Holyrood in a furiously ridden three days, and before the week was out Scotland's king was officially England's also. By early April James was on his way to London, bringing with him his favourites from the Scottish court, which somewhat alienated the English courtiers. In July he was crowned on that Stone of Destiny that Edward I had seized from Scone.

The full century between the Union of the Crowns and the Union of the Parliaments was rich in events decisive for Scotland's future. By the end of that time there came about the change that 'provincialized' the country – the change from government by its own kings and councils to government by alien parliaments sitting in London, indifferent to the needs of the north. To that state of affairs Scotland herself contributed, in this period chiefly through the passionate pursuit of a religious ideal that was truly magnificent but never practically possible. The real tragedy of that effort was that it united in a purpose doomed to failure almost the entire nation.

It is easy to overestimate the importance of the Union of 1603 and to forget that it was nothing more than a Union of the Crowns. Scotland remained, just as much as England, an independent sovereign state, with its own parliament and Privy Council, its own courts of law and national church. As yet Scotland, like England, had no standing army. When in the second half of the century a standing army was raised it was recruited in Scotland, commanded by Scotsmen and maintained out of the Scottish revenues. The customs systems of the two kingdoms were distinct, and the Union did not affect the commercial treaties between France and Scotland. But a heavy price had to be paid for this independence. In the eyes of the English law every Scotsman was a foreigner who could enjoy none of the privileges of citizenship, a tariff wall hampered the trade between the two countries, and Scotsmen were excluded from the English colonies. In these circumstances the closer connection involved a greater risk of friction. King James VI of Scotland and I of England was alive to this danger, aware that where there had been two kings before there could be two again, and set his heart on a real union. Commissioners nominated by the two parliaments drew up a Treaty of Union but neither parliament was keen. The king obtained a decision from the English judges that those born after the Union were naturalized subjects of both kingdoms, and with that he had to be content. Meantime James had announced that in future he was to be known as the King of Great Britain, France and Ireland, and ordered the same coinage and the same flag to be used in both kingdoms.

During the greater part of the seventeenth century, then, the sole link between the two kingdoms was the sovereign. It followed that the sovereign must have full control of the executive of the smaller kingdom if friction between the two countries was to be avoided. This is what happened. The Privy Council usurped more and more of the power of parliament, and both parliament and Privy Council existed simply to carry out James's wishes. The members of the Council were nominally appointed by the king in parliament; in reality they were chosen by James alone, while before the end of his reign a blow was struck at the independence of parliament. The real business of parliament was done by the Lords of the Articles, who, with the exception of the high officials, were chosen in equal numbers by their respective estates.

After the introduction into the Scottish church of bishops with a place in parliament James gave orders that the Lords of the Articles were to be chosen in a different way. The nobles were first to elect eight bishops; the bishops were then to elect eight nobles; finally bishops and nobles were to choose eight 'barons' (the name given to the county members) and eight burgesses. The eight officers of state completed the committee. When we remember that the bishops were appointed by James the meaning of the new scheme is apparent.

With one great exception James's paternal rule was a success. In the Border country – no longer 'the Borders' but 'the middle shires' – the inhabitants suddenly became peaceable and law-abiding, for Sir William Cranstoun at the head of twenty-five well-armed horsemen scoured the country from Jedburgh to Annan, making 'a quick dispatche of a grite many notable and notorious thevis and villanes by putting thame to present death without preceeding tryall.' The King's Guard, too, was transformed into a sort of mounted police, who made the sentence of outlawry more than a legal fiction.

At the same time a serious attempt was made to pacify the Highlands. In 1609 the leading chiefs met Bishop Knox at Iona and agreed to the Band of Icolmkill. Churches were to be repaired and more ministers introduced; the chiefs were to send their sons to be educated in the Lowlands; bards and beggars were to be suppressed. While the establishment of inns was recommended the importation of wines and brandies was forbidden. It was a step in the right direction, the first attempt at constructive reform instead of simple repression; but it was not nearly sufficient. Three years later Orkney and Shetland were finally annexed to the Scottish crown, but in 1614 serious rebellions broke out in both Orkney and the Western Isles. On the whole, however, Scotland was more tranquil in the second half of James VI's reign than it had been since the days of James IV.

Only in one matter did James blunder badly in his treatment of Scotland, and even then the deluge did not come in his day. He had succeeded in appointing bishops, and these bishops had taken their seats in parliament. He had more than once postponed the meetings of the General Assembly, but he had not transformed the Church of Scotland into an episcopal church. The bishops had no special function in the church. In the provincial synods and presbyteries they had no authority over their fellow ministers. To strengthen the hands of the bishops and to bring the ceremonial of the Scottish church into some degree of conformity with the English ritual was the object of James's ecclesiastical policy during the last twenty-two years of his reign.

As before he 'walked delicately', waited for his opportunity to make a false move and then seized it. It soon came. A General Assembly had been appointed to meet in Aberdeen on 2 July 1605 but had afterwards been postponed. In spite of this a handful of ministers assembled. A letter from the Privy Council was given to them by the Laird of Lauriston warning them of the king's displeasure if they persisted in holding an Assembly. The ministers, arguing that they had no right to consider the letter until they were constituted as an Assembly, appointed a Moderator and declared the Assembly duly constituted. No business was done beyond adjourning the Assembly until September, and the ministers quietly dispersed. The Council summoned the offending ministers to appear

**148**

before it. They protested that the Privy Council was not competent to judge an ecclesiastical cause and declined to appear. The king retaliated by ordering six of them to be tried for treason. The offenders were found guilty, and in October 1606 were sentenced to banishment for life.

James's path was now clear. In the summer of 1606 he had persuaded parliament to repeal the Act of 1587 whereby the Church lands had been annexed to the crown and thus provided the new bishops with a revenue befitting their station.

The next step was taken three years later, when an Assembly met in Glasgow. The utmost care was taken to make the results of its deliberations agreeable to James. The Assembly declared that although it was expedient that a General Assembly should meet every year it could meet only if the king gave his consent. Bishops were to become moderators of the diocesan synods; without their consent no minister could be ordained or deposed, nor could any sentence of excommunication be pronounced. The very name 'presbytery' was abolished, 'as odious to his Majestie'. Three bishops straightaway went to London to be consecrated by their Anglican brethren. Two years later the creation of a Court of High Commission for the Province of St Andrews and a second for the Province of Glasgow completed the ruin of the Presbyterian system.

On 16 May 1617, while the cannon thundered from the castle, James rode into Edinburgh on his only visit to Scotland after the Union of the Crowns. The very next morning the Anglican service was said in the chapel of Holyrood. The chief object of James's visit was now apparent. At a convention of ministers that assembled at St Andrews in July he berated the bishops for their lack of energy in furthering his designs and submitted five articles suggesting changes in the ceremonial of the church. Private baptism and private communion were to be allowed, communicants were to kneel as they received the sacrament, confirmation was to be instituted, and the great festivals of the Church were to be observed. The convention declared that it was not competent to deal with such questions and remitted the matter to an Assembly that met at St Andrews at the end of October, almost three months after the king had left Scotland. The Assembly would do no more than give a qualified assent to two of the articles. Another Assembly that met at Perth in August 1618 saw the matter completed. Spottiswoode, the Archbishop of St Andrews, declared that it was simply a question of pleasing or displeasing the king. Although he disliked the articles himself, yet for the sake of peace he urged the Assembly to give way to the king. The articles were adopted and three years later were confirmed by the Scottish parliament.

James had gone too far this time. From the beginning the articles were disregarded, and the bishops were neither willing nor able to punish breaches of the law with severity. Churches where the communicant was required to kneel were deserted; in others the sacrament was administered both to those who sat and those who knelt. In one church the sacrament is said to have been administered in five different ways. Few attended communion on Easter Sunday; scores of shops in the main streets of Edinburgh stood open on Christmas Day.

The death of King James in 1625 brought to the throne a man who was absolutely ignorant of Scottish affairs. Although Charles I had been born at Dunfermline he had left Scotland when he was three years old, and since then had not set foot in the country. He could not know that the success of his father's ecclesiastical policy was the result of a quarter of a century of cautious diplomacy, that no change was made by the royal authority alone, and that although the bulk of the nation had submitted to a moderate episcopacy the submission had been reluctantly made. Still less did he understand that even the Scottish bishops looked on episcopal government as expedient but not essential, and that some of them detested the ceremonies that meant so much to Archbishop Laud in England and his fellows.

Charles I brought to the observance of his own religion a perhaps too Scottish fervour. His mistake was his effort to enforce his own narrow Anglicanism throughout his kingdoms in a logical but misguided drive for uniformity. The Scots Kirk would have none of it. When they found their own Presbyterianism echoed in Charles's rebel parliament there was an Anglo-Scottish band against the king. This was the Solemn League and Covenant. Its agreement as a treaty was that in alliance with the rebel English parliament, and in return for the bare expenses of a Scottish army fighting in England, Presbyterianism was to be made the religion of England and Ireland as well as Scotland. In other words, the Scots were to play that part in England that Charles had played in Scotland. They were to force on the country a form of religion for which the majority of the inhabitants had no affection.

To anything but a state of acute religious exaltation the futility of this bargain would have been apparent. The other two countries were not less likely than Scotland to be stubborn about their religion, and England was not Presbyterian in the Scottish sense, while Ireland was not Presbyterian at all but determinedly Roman Catholic. The Covenanted Scots carried out their side of the bargain and fought sturdily in England against the king, although harassed at home by the magnificent campaigns of Montrose as the King's Lieutenant in Scotland. But with the appearance and increasing triumph of the genius of Cromwell the Scots became less necessary to the English arms, and English loyalty to the Covenant grew less and less noticeable. In that split Charles I saw an opportunity and surrendered to the Scots, but the concessions he was ready to make did not go quite far enough to offset renewed bargaining between the Scottish and English Covenanters, bargaining in which the king became a pawn. The Scots handed him over, on the promise of his safety and a furtherance of part of the Covenant's purposes. But there figured also in the bargain an English payment of part of the Scots army's allowance (a part was all that was ever paid), and the appearance that Charles had been sold for cash was not passed over. 'Traitor Scot,' ran the jingle, 'Sold his King for a groat.'

When the moderate Covenanters realized that their hopes for a Presbyterian settlement in England would be better served by having a legitimate sovereign than by the turbulent Cromwell, they rallied in support of Charles. By the 'Engagement' as it was called, Charles undertook to establish Presbyterianism in England for three years, and although he still refused to sign the Covenant or enforce it on his subjects he promised to confirm it in parliament. In return for this the Scots promised to put their army at his disposal. The Engagement was a failure, however, and the defeat of the Royalist army at Preston in 1648 sealed the king's fate. Cromwell was soon able to coerce parliament and the more hesitant of the Presbyterians into bringing Charles to trial for high treason against the people.

Although Charles repeatedly refused to recognize the court he had the sentence of death pronounced against him. All interposition being in vain, he was beheaded before the Banqueting House in Whitehall, meeting his fate with an admirable obstinacy that seemed dignified and courageous.

The execution of Charles I sent a thrill of horror throughout Scotland. Charles II was at once proclaimed by the parliament, and even the dominant minority thought that the young king might be invited to Scotland. But Charles did not intend to become a Presbyterian and a Covenanter unless it was absolutely necessary. There was just a chance that a Royalist rising in the Highlands might be successful, and in the spring of 1650 Montrose was sent on what he knew was a hopeless venture. Yet he went gladly; ready, he said, 'to abandon still my life to search my death for the interests of your Majesty's honour and service.' With a few hundred Orcadians and foreign mercenaries he landed in Caithness, but hardly a man joined him, and when he reached Carbisdale, in Ross, his timorous levies were easily dispersed by a small force under Colonel Strachan. Montrose escaped but was captured soon afterwards and taken to Edinburgh where he was hanged on 21 May, his last words being 'God have mercy on this afflicted country'. After his death he was dismembered. His head was placed on a spike on the Tolbooth of Edinburgh and his limbs taken to Stirling, Perth, Aberdeen and Glasgow. Charles II, capable of any dissimulation in order to further his own cause, had disowned him.

A month later Charles, having signed the two Covenants, made his appearance in Scotland, and towards the end of July Cromwell crossed the Border. In the face of this danger the Duke of Argyll's party acted as if it had been stricken with insanity. The Act of Classes was introduced, which divided all those who had supported the royalist cause or the Engagement or who had merely 'neglected to protest' into three groups: the first were deprived of holding any office for life,

**153**

the second for ten years, the third for five. It deprived the once splendid army of its steadiest soldiers and most experienced leaders.

Cromwell's intention was to force a way into Edinburgh, but his path was barred by the Scottish army, about twice the size of his own, under David Leslie. The whole of August was spent in fruitless marching and countermarching, for the Scottish army, moving along interior lines, could always keep itself between Cromwell and Edinburgh. Finally Cromwell resolved to give up the attempt on Edinburgh and lead his men along the coast to Berwick. On 1 September Dunbar was reached, but Leslie seized Doon Hill and the narrow passage of Cockburnspath and barred the way to England. Cromwell was trapped. If he resolved to fight, the enemy, besides outnumbering him by two to one, had all the advantages of ground. If he tried to embark his men on the ships he was certain to lose heavily. Fortunately for him, Leslie had to do the bidding of a Committee of the Estates, 'who were weary of lying in the fields' and 'called to him to fall on', so Leslie had to abandon his strong military position and advance towards the English and be defeated. Dunbar was not a decisive battle, however, although it allowed Cromwell to hold Edinburgh Castle and Lothian. The Scots regrouped around Stirling Castle, barring the way to the north.

Many of the more precise Presbyterians now saw that if the honour of Scotland was to be preserved the services of every man willing to fight for his country were required. Many were convinced, however, that the 'singular piece of dispensation' was due, not to their intolerance, but to their laxity, and in October they presented a Remonstrance to the Committee of the Estates in which they disowned King Charles, rebuked the Committee for walking more by the rule of

**154**

policy than piety, and demanded that all who had fought for Charles I and all who had suggested cooperating with them should be removed from places of trust. They organized a separate army that was meant to menace the loyalists more than the English, but this force allowed itself to be beaten rather than cooperate with the main army. This defeat freed the hands of the moderate party. On the first day of 1651 the king was crowned at Scone, and in June the Act of Classes was formally repealed.

Now that the Act of Classes was abolished fresh recruits poured in, until Leslie commanded a far finer army than those destroyed at Preston and Dunbar. Cromwell knew that until this force was destroyed he could not hope to be master of the whole of Scotland. He knew, too, that he would have difficulty in forcing it from its 'lock' at Stirling. He therefore decided to cross the Forth and strike at the Scottish base at Perth. On 20 July Lambert drove the Scottish garrison from the fortifications of Inverkeithing. On 2 August Perth was seized by Cromwell. But news came that the main Scottish army was now marching hotfoot for England, and, leaving Monck to finish the northern campaign, he pursued them to Worcester where the Scottish army was completely destroyed. Every leader of note, except Charles himself, who had managed to flee to France, was in Cromwell's hands.

Meantime Monck had not been idle. Stirling had been captured, Dundee stormed and sacked, and one of Monck's officers, by arresting the remnant of the Committee of the Estates at Alyth, put an end to organized government in Scotland. For the next seven years Scotland, like England, lay at the feet of Cromwell. Although a royalist rising in the Highlands caused some trouble before it was suppressed in 1654, 'in no time,' says Bishop Burnet, 'the Highlands were kept in better order than during the usurpation.' A permanent garrison of several thousand men was maintained in Scotland, and new and powerful fortresses at Inverness, Inverlochy, Ayr, Perth, and Leith enabled General Monck to hold the country in a grip of iron. The once omnipotent General Assembly vanished, broken up in 1653 on the suspicion of being in communication with the northern rebels, and with its disappearance the ecclesiastical warfare ended for a time.

But Cromwell did not intend to leave Scotland in the position of a conquered province. In 1652 Scotland was united to England, and in the Instrument of Government it was stipulated that thirty Scottish members should sit in the Protectorate Parliament. The Privy Council was replaced by a small Council of State, seven Commissioners – 'kinless loons' who refused to be bribed – administered justice, and Scottish merchants could now trade with England or the English colonies without restriction. But the union was an artificial one. The majority of the members of parliament and six out of eight of the Council of State were Englishmen, and although trade increased taxation increased too, for the greater part of the cost of the army of occupation was met by the inhabitants of Scotland. Men longed for a change, little knowing what the change would bring.

The restoration of Charles II ended eight years of enforced union and was hailed in Scotland with wild enthusiasm. The members of the first Restoration parliament caroused so long at night that morning sittings were abandoned and a custom centuries old was broken. The Presbyterians, for their part, did not look to the future with apprehension. Although there was little chance of Charles remaining faithful to the Covenants, it was improbable that a prince who 'did not think that there was either sincerity or chastity in the world out of principle'

**156**

would become a scourge of heresy, and when a few months after the Restoration he assured the Presbytery of Edinburgh that he would protect the church as established by law the grateful ministers enshrined his letter in a silver box.

Charles II never revisited Scotland, and his rule there was administered by John Middleton (created an earl in 1656) as his Royal Commissioner to Scotland and by the Earl of Lauderdale, nicknamed 'The King of Scotland', who was his Secretary of State. Lauderdale, had had more love for Presbyterianism than for Episcopacy. When Charles 'spoke to him to let that go, for it was not a religion for gentlemen', he obeyed only as far as outward appearance went and tried to persuade Charles not to meddle with the Scottish church. Although the English parliament spoke smoothly, he assured Charles that 'that was only the honeymoon' and he would soon find that the surest bulwark of the throne was a contented Scotland. But Charles was overruled by James Sharp, once the minister of Crail, who had been sent to London to represent the moderate Presbyterians and was working hard for the re-establishment of Episcopacy.

The first sign of the coming trouble was seen in the proceedings of the parliament that met on New Year's Day in 1661, known as the 'Drunken Parliament', which passed the Rescissory Act that annulled all the legislation since 1633, including the Acts of the 1641 parliament at which Charles I had presided in person, the Acts of the parliament that ratified the Engagement and those of Charles II's earlier parliaments. By this Act, Parliament set fetters on itself, for not only was the abolition of the Committee of the Articles annulled but the destruction at one sweep of the whole work of parliament for more than a quarter of a century was a constitutional innovation of the most disquieting kind.

**157**

Even more disturbing were the innovations in the church. In September the Privy Council announced that the church as settled by law meant the Episcopal church of 1633, and before the end of the year Sharp, now Archbishop of St Andrews, Robert Leighton, Bishop of Dunblane, and two other Scottish bishops went to London to be consecrated after the manner of the Church of England. The Drunken Parliament in its second session, in the summer of 1662, brought the bishops back to their old paces, declared the Covenant illegal and passed an Act of Indemnity. A few, like Argyll, Johnston of Warriston, and one or two of the more fanatical ministers, were absolutely excluded from the benefits of the indemnity and were executed; over eight hundred persons were to be pardoned only on condition that they paid heavy fines. Another Act, introducing lay patronage, which had been abolished by the parliament of 1649, caused a conflagration. For the last twenty years every vacancy in the Church of Scotland had been filled by a candidate appointed by the majority, or an overbearing minority, of the congregation. It was now enacted that all ministers who had been placed since 1649 must receive the charge again from the lay patron of the church and the bishop of the diocese or else resign. The last day for submission was 13 February 1663. When that day came, almost three hundred ministers, about a third of the clergy of the whole kingdom, had resigned their charges.

It was a fatal blunder. Even though the bulk of the deprived ministers belonged to the most illiberal section of the clergy, even though they had few supporters outside the southwest, the government had created a problem that two rebellions were to leave unsolved. The pity of it is that the government was contending for so little that one is at a loss to know why it should have contended at all. Although no General Assembly had been held since 1653, the synods and presbyteries were allowed to retain their former power and no attempt was made by the government to impose a liturgy or any innovations in ceremonial upon the church.

The events of the next few years showed the folly of attempting to gain converts to a policy of moderation by the use of compulsion. The places of the ejected ministers were given to the first candidates who offered their services, in most cases half-educated youths from the north of Scotland. The congregations found fault not only with the preaching of the 'curates', as they christened them, but with their mode of life. Few troubled to listen to their sermons, and when the ejected ministers preached under the open sky they found the bulk of their flock gathered round them. The government replied by imposing fines, not only on those who attended conventicles, as these open-air meetings were called, but also on those who stayed away from church, and masters who would not give information about non-conforming servants were held equally guilty. Troops of dragoons extracted the fines from the Whigs in a somewhat rough-and-ready fashion. Under this petty persecution the temper of the people in the West Country became sullen. Rumours of defeat at sea, stories of the destruction wrought by the Great Fire, led them to believe that the government was tottering to a fall and on 15 November 1666 a rebellion in Galloway began. The rebels advanced on Edinburgh but could find no support in the eastern counties. They got as far as Colinton, within a few miles of Edinburgh, but as no word of encouragement came from the capital they resolved to cross the Pentlands and make for home. On 26 November they were overtaken by regular troops at Rullion Green and scattered after a brisk encounter. For months after the battle the search for the fugitives continued. More than thirty were executed, ten being hanged on one gibbet at Edinburgh, while at least two were tortured to death. Those who were spared were shipped to the plantations in Barbados.

The zeal of the two churchmen, Archbishop Sharp of St Andrews and Professor Burnet of Glasgow, for the persecution of the Whigs made them unpopular with many who did not hold the extreme views of the victims. The Whigs would gladly have re-established the religious tyranny that briefly flourished after the collapse of the Engagement. They suffered martyrdom but they would have willingly martyred others who did not share their opinions. For two decades such scenes were to be repeated, despite occasional attempts to compromise on the government side.

Lauderdale's plan was to tempt the ejected ministers back to the church. If he did not win them all over, he would at least succeed in splitting the ranks of the malcontents. In the summer of 1669 he persuaded the king to issue his first Letter of Indulgence. Ejected ministers who had lived peaceably were allowed to return to their parishes if the Privy Council gave its consent, but unless they promised to take their benefices from their bishops they were to receive only a portion of the revenue. When parliament met in October Lauderdale, now Lord High Commissioner, buttressed up the Indulgence by securing the passage of an Act that declared the absolute supremacy of the king in all ecclesiastical affairs, far too heavy a price to pay for the submission of forty-two ministers.

In 1670 Lauderdale secured the passage of a Bill making attendance at a conventicle treasonable and preaching at it punishable by death. Even the king blamed Lauderdale for exceeding his instructions and protested that 'bloody laws did no good'. The issue of the second Letter of Indulgence in

1672 took much of the terror from this 'clanking act'. Ninety deprived ministers were appointed to fifty-eight parishes on condition that each one remained in the parish allotted. By settling the deprived ministers in pairs the plan was that the disaffection would be confined to a comparatively small area and at the same time their congregations would discover that Presbyterianism was twice as expensive as Episcopacy.

A series of statutes goaded the western Whigs into madness. In 1673 it was ordained that landowners should be fined one-fourth of their yearly revenue for every conventicle held on their lands. In the following year, and again in 1677, they were made responsible for the conduct of their tenants and servants. Early in 1678 a disorderly army of six thousand Highlanders and three thousand Lowland militia was quartered in the southwest for five weeks, and a few months later a new tax of £1,800,000 Scots, payable within five years, was imposed by parliament. A general conflagration could not be long delayed. On 3 May 1679, Archbishop Sharp, whom the average Covenanter regarded as the chief instigator of the policy of repression, was dragged from his coach and butchered near St Andrews, and on the king's birthday a party of horsemen rode into Rutherglen, stamped out the bonfires, and burned copies of every Act condemning the Covenant.

Worse was to follow. A few days later John Graham of Claverhouse, the most able and energetic officer in the Scottish army, rode out to disperse a large conventicle. He came upon the Covenanters at Drumclog, near Loudoun Hill. Well armed and skilfully posted on the farther side of a marsh, they far outnumbered his company of horsemen, but Claverhouse resolved to engage them. A few shots were exchanged and both sides advanced to the attack, but only the Covenanters knew the paths through the bog. The royal troops, flounder-

ing in the soft ground, could not withstand the rush of the
enthusiasts, and Claverhouse and the remainder of his men
were soon riding hard to Glasgow. The garrison evacuated
the city, and two days after the battle it fell into the hands of
the insurgents. The Duke of Monmouth, illegitimate son of
Charles II, was at once dispatched to take command of the
royal forces in Scotland. Meantime the insurgents threw away
their chances of success by quarrelling among themselves.
Everyone was fighting for the Covenant, every one was opposed to the Indulgence, but a small and very energetic faction refused to have any dealings with the indulged clergy
and wished to convert the rising into a war against the king,
while the larger division was willing to discuss matters with
the indulged ministers and considered that the Covenant en-
joined loyalty to the sovereign. The moderate party was on
the point of opening negotiations with Monmouth when on
22 June the royal army appeared and a battle became inevitable. The Covenanters had the advantage in numbers and position. Between them and their enemies flowed the Clyde,
spanned by Bothwell Bridge, and the bridge and the houses
beside it were held by their musketeers. Until the bridge was
captured the royal cavalry would be useless, but the two factions preferred victory in debate to victory in the field. No
supports were sent to the party that obstinately held the
bridge, the gallant defenders – most of them drawn from the
moderate party – were forced back, and Claverhouse's horsemen were soon slashing and slaying among the undisciplined
rabble. The victory was complete. A thousand prisoners, almost a quarter of the whole army, were driven to Edinburgh,
where for five months they were penned up in an enclosure
in Greyfriars Churchyard, open to the sky. They were offered
their freedom if they would promise not to take up arms

against the king. Some four hundred refused this clemency and were shipped to the West Indian plantations, but the vessel bearing them was wrecked off Orkney and most of the captives perished. Seven of the leaders of the insurrection were hanged in the Grassmarket in Edinburgh.

The only Presbyterians who now remained in arms was a tiny minority of extremists who had declared war not only against Episcopacy but also against the king, and who from the name of their leader, Richard Cameron, who was killed in a skirmish at Aird's Moss, began to be known as Cameronians. In 1684 the Cameronians issued the *Apologetical Declaration*, in which they announced that they were justified in killing all who sought to hunt them down and gave effect to their threat by strangling a trooper and murdering a curate.

But the excesses of the Cameronians by no means clear the government of the blame of being unduly repressive in not discriminating between rebels who actually remained in arms and rebels who, cowed by their defeat, were now living at peace with all men. It continued to treat all Presbyterians as if they were potential rebels, an ungenerous and criminal folly. At the end of 1679, however, the Catholic Duke of York replaced Lauderdale as Commissioner, the weak and ferocious Burnet became Archbishop of St Andrews, and the baiting of the Presbyterians went merrily on.

In 1681 parliament declared that the sovereign need not be a Protestant and strengthened the Duke of York's position further by imposing a 'Test' upon all who held office. They were required to remain faithful to the Protestant religion as defined in the first Confession of Faith, to renounce the Covenant, to promise to defend all the king's rights and treat of no matter, civil or ecclesiastical, without his consent. The Test Act was contradictory. By no ingenuity could absolute obedience to the king be reconciled with the doctrines laid down in the Confession of Faith, but as few members of parliament and none of the bishops had read the Confession that objection did not keep the Test out of the statute book. But some men were more scrupulous. Eighty ministers, many of them Episcopalians, refused to take the Test and were deposed. The Earl of Argyll declared that he took the Test so far 'as it was consistent with itself'. For this he was tried, found guilty of treason and was saved from the scaffold only by escaping from prison and taking refuge in Holland.

This parliament was not content with striking at offenders of comparatively high rank. It declared that all ministers must provide their bishops with lists of those who did not attend church, and Claverhouse and other officers were sent out to enforce the penalties of non-attendance. Soon the churches were crowded, even in places where no service had been held for years, but the men 'were either talking or sleeping all the while', and the women, who had not been mentioned in the Act, stayed at home.

A few months later the Privy Council and such circuit courts as it should appoint were authorized by royal proclamation to summon and deal with all persons who had harboured or conversed with rebels before May 1683. In the following year every Presbyterian minister in the kingdom was ejected from his parish. Almost all refused to promise not to preach and were imprisoned. The Privy Council answered the *Apologetical Declaration* by declaring that whoever refused to repudiate it would be put to death without a trial, and in December 1684 it was proclaimed that no person over sixteen must travel without a certificate that he had disowned the Declaration.

The death of Charles II in 1685 did nothing to mitigate the

**164**

severity of the government, for which, in fact, the new king had been mainly responsible. The first parliament of the reign, indeed, sought to gain James VII and II's favour by declaring that it was treasonable to take the Covenants and that all who attended a field conventicle and the preachers at a house conventicle were liable to be put to death. But after a rebellion by the Earl of Argyll, returned from Holland, to replace the openly Catholic James VII with the Duke of Monmouth had ended with the capture and death of the half-hearted leader, it became apparent that James's ecclesiastical policy was inspired less by hatred of Presbyterianism than by zeal for Catholicism. The Chancellor, the Earl of Perth, became a Catholic and shocked the pope by marrying his cousin a few weeks after the death of his first wife. His brother, Viscount Melfort, and the Earl of Moray also professed themselves converts to 'the King's religion', as the Scottish bishops called it. But few followed their example. The Duke of Queensberry, for example, rather than turn Catholic, suffered himself to be deprived of the offices of Treasurer and Lord High Commissioner and was replaced in command of Edinburgh Castle by the Catholic Duke of Gordon.

A few weeks later, in April 1686, parliament met for its second session. The king's purpose was now apparent. He urged parliament to repeal the laws against Catholics. Parliament refused and was dismissed. James now announced that as parliament declined to cooperate with him his hands were free, and in September he issued his first Letter of Indulgence, suspending all laws against Catholics. A second Letter was issued in February 1687, and a third Letter, published in July, gave complete freedom of worship to Presbyterians. Most Presbyterians accepted the Indulgence gladly, for their spirit had been broken in the long struggle.

**165**

# CHAPTER XIII

# REVOLUTION AND UNION OF THE PARLIAMENTS

In the train of events that drove James into exile and made Mary, James's elder daughter, and her husband, William of Orange, rulers of England, Scotland had no direct share, but it was evident that the sympathies of the average Lowlander were not with James. In December 1688 a mob broke into the Chapel Royal at Holyrood, which had lately been fitted up as a Catholic chapel, and purged it as thoroughly as Knox's 'raschall multitude' could have done. The Chancellor, Perth, disguised himself and hid on a ship, but he was dragged out and clapped into prison. On Christmas Day the 'rabbling' of the 'curates' began. The Presbyterians of the western counties were in no forgiving mood. In many places they invaded the manse, marched the minister in mock procession through the village, tore his gown and finally drove him from the parish.

The Episcopal clergy were at the parting of the ways. William was guided in Scottish affairs by his chaplain, William Carstares, who had once borne the torture of the thumbscrews without betraying his prince's secrets, and Carstares was a moderate Presbyterian. But William was neither a Presbyterian nor an Episcopalian. He did not care whether Presbyterianism or Episcopacy prevailed in Scotland so long as the country remained tranquil, and if the Episcopal clergy had pledged themselves to support him he would have dealt with them generously, but the sympathies of the Episcopalians were in most cases with the exiled king.

The Convention of the Estates that met in Edinburgh on 14 March 1689 assumed powers to which no Scottish parliament had ever laid claim. In the Claim of Right it declared the right to depose the sovereign, recited the fundamental laws of the kingdom that James had broken and offered the crown to William and Mary, She as a daughter of James VII and he as a grandson of Charles I, both offered an element of Stewart legitimacy, but William was the dominant figure in their joint sovereignty. The offer was loaded with an important condition: Episcopacy must be abolished. It was certain now that Episcopacy would fail, but William recognized that to replace it by a persecuting Presbyterianism would perpetuate the old evil under a new name. He took the oath to uphold the religion of Scotland with the reservation that he would never be a persecutor. Meantime the Episcopalians were helping to resolve William's perplexities. For refusing to discharge their parishioners from obedience to King James, nearly two hundred ministers were deprived of their churches.

The cause of James was not to perish without a final struggle. A few months after his flight, Graham of Claverhouse, now Viscount Dundee, raised the royalist standard and defeated an English army at Killiecrankie. Dundee was killed in the battle, and without his leadership the rebellion's momentum was lost. A further battle took place in August the same year at Dunkeld, but the outcome was indecisive although both sides claimed victory. The rising in Scotland rumbled on for a further ten months until the remaining rebels were overcome at Cromdale in early 1690.

**167**

The same year, 1690, saw the establishment of the Church of Scotland as it now exists. The Duke of Hamilton had been succeeded as Commissioner by the Presbyterian Earl of Melville, who, soon after the Scots parliament met for its second session, ratified two Acts that Hamilton had rejected. The first abolished the royal supremacy in ecclesiastical causes, the second restored to their parishes all ministers who had been ejected since 1661. A more important Act was passed on 7 June. The Confession of Faith, issued by the Assembly of Divines at Westminster in 1647, was adopted as the standard of belief in the Scottish church, and government by presbyteries, synods and Assemblies was declared to be 'the only government of Christ's Church within this kingdom'. All parishes from which Episcopalians had been expelled were declared vacant, and a day later lay patronage was abolished.

The danger was that the Presbyterians would in their turn become persecutors. It is true that the old ministers who were reinstated had in their adversity learned moderation, but the younger ministers 'broke out into a most extravagant way of proceeding', and the 'rabbling' that had hitherto been confined to the southwest now spread to the north. Nor was this outbreak simply an expression of mob fury, for the General Assembly that met in the autumn of 1690 appointed two Commissioners with powers to examine any minister and expel him if they thought fit. William intervened to stop this petty persecution and several times tried to persuade the Scottish Episcopal clergy to enter the Church of Scotland. But neither Presbyterian nor Episcopalian would yield an inch, and the ideal of a Church of Scotland that would include every Protestant in Scotland had to be abandoned. Happily it was recognized now that true religious unity could not be produced by compulsion, and in 1695 the Scottish

**168**

parliament declared that Episcopal clergymen who had taken the Oath of Allegiance and recognized William as king *de jure* as well as *de facto* would not be molested provided they took no share in the government of the church. More than a hundred took advantage of this Act. In 1710 as many as a hundred and thirteen Episcopalians still held livings in Scotland.

The century and a half of religious strife had ended in the establishment of a church that was a state church only in the sense that it was recognized and supported by the state. It no longer sought to dominate the state. The state, on the other hand, gave up the attempt to control its doctrine and ritual.

The accession of William III to the throne of Scotland had results less desirable than the establishment of Presbyterianism. Under the Stewart regime, as we have seen, Scotland preserved a nominal independence at the cost of a very real dependence on the sovereign. Much of the work formerly done by parliament was transferred to the Privy Council, and parliament itself was not free, for the drafting and discussion of legislation was the special province of the Committee of the Articles, from which the curious system of election excluded any man who was likely to disregard the wishes of the king. An Act of the Scottish parliament of 1690 abolished the Committee of the Articles. The danger that threatened now was that the parliament would make use of its freedom to pursue a distinctively national policy and that sooner or later the national jealousies that had smouldered since 1603 would burst into flame. And William III, for all his great gifts, for all his anxiety to deal even justice, was in some respects unfitted for the task now thrust upon him. He had never set foot in Scotland. For his information about the country he was dependent upon men like Bishop Burnet and Carstares, who, fortunately, were remarkable for prudence and moderation.

**169**

He was not specially interested in Scotland – his preoccupation with the ambitions of Louis XIV prevented that – and he frequently let business accumulate and then signed a mass of papers without stopping to consider their import. Even those Scots who had favoured the Revolution regarded him with respect rather than affection, while, if he should blunder, swarms of Jacobite politicians and pamphleteers were ready to point the moral.

Once he did blunder badly. In 1691 the Earl of Breadalbane, head of one of the branches of the great Clan Campbell, undertook to pacify the Highlands at the moderate cost of £12,000. With this sum he would buy the allegiance of the most important chiefs. The government supplied him with the money, but it was whispered in the Highlands that a man might have a share of the spoil even though Breadalbane knew him to be a Jacobite and that the earl meant to keep the greater part of the money to himself. The result was that the chiefs demanded more than the earl had intended to give them and left him without a penny.

Conspicuous among the chiefs who had ruined Breadalbane's scheme was Alexander MacDonald, chief of a small but warlike clan that dwelt in Glencoe, one of the wildest and most inaccessible of the West Highland glens. The clan had a record of crimes of violence to its name and had frequently given the Clan Campbell, its nearest neighbour, good cause to remember it. When it was announced that every chief in the Highlands should take the oath of allegiance before January 1692, it was only to be expected that Alexander MacDonald would refuse to commit himself until the very last minute. In the last days of December his fears got the better of him, and he set out for Fort William, the stronghold recently rebuilt by General Mackay to overawe the Highlands. But the commanding officer there was not a magistrate and could do no more than send him on to Inveraray. Deep snowdrifts blocked the passes and prevented him reaching the county town before 6 January 1692. There, after his explanation had been heard, the magistrate allowed him to take the oath, and he returned to the glen well content.

Meanwhile Breadalbane had gone to London, satisfied with nothing less than the extirpation of the obnoxious clan, and he found a ready ally in one of the Secretaries of State, Sir James Dalrymple. A proclamation ordering the extirpation of the MacDonalds of Glencoe was drawn up by Dalrymple and presented to the king, who signed and countersigned it. The plotters thus made the king responsible for whatever they might do. The order was dispatched to Scotland, and on 1 February Captain Campbell of Glenlyon entered Glencoe at the head of his company. Highland hospitality soon conquered the fear of the stranger. The soldiers were billeted in the huts of the clansmen, and for almost a fortnight the slayers and their appointed victims spent the time in merriment. At five o'clock on the morning of 13 February the crack of musket shots let the MacDonalds know why the soldiers had come among them. Many were warned by the sounds and fled in time, but thirty-eight, including the chief and his two sons, were shot down. How many of the fugitives perished among the snow-clad hills will never be known. Had swords been used instead of firearms, had the troops co-operating with Campbell's company been at their stations in time, not a soul would have escaped.

It was a deed of remarkable ferocity and treachery, although by no means without a parallel in the bloodstained history of the Scottish Highlands. Yet months passed before it created any stir in the Lowlands. Only when the Jacobite

**171**

politicians saw how William had played into their hands, and in pamphlet after pamphlet cited the massacre and William's slowness in calling the murderers to account as a revelation of his true character, did the demand for an inquiry become general. Not until the following year did the king appoint a committee to investigate the affair. The findings of this body proved to be somewhat disconcerting and so many persons of high rank appeared to be involved that William tried to let the matter drop. This mistaken clemency only added strength to the clamour in Scotland, and in 1695 the king was forced to appoint another commission, which delivered its report to the Scottish parliament. Parliament declared that the slaying of the MacDonalds had been a barbarous massacre and, while exonerating the king from blame, asked that the offenders should be punished. Dalrymple was deprived of his office; Breadalbane was sent to prison but never brought to trial. The others escaped. The carelessness that allowed William to deliver the inhabitants of Glencoe into the hands of their hereditary enemies and his evident unwillingness to punish their murderers drove the Highlanders over to the side of the exiled king and lost him the sympathy of many of those Scotsmen who had welcomed his accession to the throne.

By now attention in Scotland had shifted to consideration of the ill-fated Darien Scheme. Scotland, excluded from any part of the wealth generated in England from its trade with its far-flung colonies, decided to establish a colony of its own, a cherished dream of William Paterson, the Scottish founder of the Bank of England. An Act passed in 1693 for the purpose of encouraging foreign trade, together with the setting up of the Company of Scotland, with powers granted by parliament to found new colonies, laid the foundations of the scheme. The site for the proposed colony lay in Spanish territory, and Spain did not approve of the founding of a 'New Caledonia' on its property. In addition, the area became a swamp in the summer, infested with fever. The expeditions to Darien were catastrophic. Fever claimed the lives of many of the colonists, and the English possessions in the West Indies refused supplies to the stricken colony, which was subsequently closed down by Spanish troops. It was a financial disaster that was widely felt and certainly did nothing to improve Anglo-Scottish relations, a development that William feared. He believed that separation of England and Scotland was inevitable unless a closer union could be effected, and even when he lay on his deathbed he implored the Commons to bring this union about.

Queen Anne repeated his advice, and in November 1702 twenty-three English commissioners and twenty-one Scots met at Whitehall to draft a treaty of union. It was plain that the English representatives were not interested in the business. Time and again meetings had to be adjourned because of their absence, and although it was agreed that the parliaments of the two countries should be joined and that Electress Sophia of Hanover should succeed to the throne they would not grant the slightest concession to Scottish merchants.

The breakdown in the negotiations had obviously affected the temper of the parliament that assembled in the early summer of the following year – the last Scottish parliament, as it afterwards proved to be. The Revolution had given it weapons that hitherto had been the exclusive property of the English parliament. It had freedom of debate, the power to decide the succession and the power to refuse supplies. These powers it resolved to use. After debates lasting for five weeks, it passed the Act of Security, declaring that unless Scotland were granted the same trading privileges as England, unless

**173**

her liberty and religion were guaranteed, the person chosen by the English government to succeed Queen Anne would not be accepted by the Scottish people. At the same time steps were to be taken to prepare the country for war. The Commissioner, the Duke of Queensberry, refused to sanction the Act. On 15 September a furious debate took place. The Estates sat far into the night, the dark, tapestry-clad hall resounded with cries of 'Liberty and no subsidy!' Members sat with their hands on their swords. The decision was taken. Since the queen would not give her assent to the Act of Security supply must be refused. Next day Queensberry prorogued parliament.

A change of government now took place. Hitherto most of the offices of state had been in the hands of the Court Party, which had usually shown itself willing to act in conjunction with the sovereign and the English ministers. Opposed to it was the Country Party – the patriots and the Jacobites. But Queensberry's failure to suppress the Act of Security, joined to his clumsy handling of a Jacobite plot, led to his fall from office and the dismissal of most of the Scottish ministers. He was succeeded by the Earl of Tweeddale, one of the leaders of the Country Party, a section of which now formed the government. Tweeddale was to endeavour to get the succession settled and opened a second session of parliament in July 1704. The change of government was a failure. The ministry had not a majority of the members behind it, and within a few days supply was definitely refused.

The danger was averted for the time by the queen giving her assent to the Act of Security, but the English parliament had still to be reckoned with. In March 1705 it passed the Aliens Act, prohibiting all imports from Scotland and declaring all Scots aliens if before the end of the year the Scottish

**174**

parliament did not come to a satisfactory conclusion regarding the succession. At the same time the queen was empowered to appoint commissioners to negotiate for a Union. But with every day the prospect of a union, or even of a continuance of peace, seemed to recede. In the spring of 1705 an English ship, the *Worcester*, put into Leith. From some careless words dropped by the crew, it appeared that they had been guilty of piracy. The rumour got out that they were responsible for the loss of a Scottish ship, and forthwith the men were arrested and tried. On the flimsiest of evidence a verdict of guilty was returned, and despite vigorous demands from the English government for a reprieve, the captain and two of his men were executed on the sands of Leith.

It was evident now that a closer union was the only alternative to war. In June the young Duke of Argyll was sent to Scotland as Lord Commissioner, and the old Court Party was reinstated. An Act for a treaty with England was introduced and debated fiercely for more than a month. Once it was rejected by three votes, but on 24 August it was safely through the first reading. Thirty-one commissioners were to draw up a treaty, but they were forbidden to meddle with the national religion. The Jacobites and other opponents of the union still felt that there was hope. If the commissioners were chosen in due proportion from every party it would be impossible for them to agree, but the Duke of Hamilton, to the amazement of his supporters, stultified their plans by urging that the commissioners should be appointed by the queen. At the same time the queen was asked to secure the repeal of the Aliens Act, and when it was rescinded by the English parliament before the end of the year the relations between the two countries became less strained.

On 16 April 1706, the Scottish and English commissioners

**175**

met in the Cockpit at Whitehall, overlooking the green spaces of St James's Park. Before a fortnight had passed the successful issue of the negotiations was assured. A federal union would have provided an ideal solution for the problem. This scheme would have left Scotland and England with separate legislatures, although matters that concerned both nations would be dealt with by joint committees or perhaps in a joint session of the two parliaments. The English representatives urged that this was too small a return for commercial equality, and eventually it was agreed that there should be only one parliament for the two nations, that a prince of the house of Hanover should succeed and that Scotland should have the same trading privileges as England.

Many questions, however, had to be decided before the Act could be completed. Equality of trading privileges meant equal liability to taxation; but the English National Debt was £17,763,842, while the Scottish debt was only about an eleventh of that amount. On the other hand, the yearly revenue of Scotland amounted to no more than £160,000, or less than a thirty-fifth of the English revenue. Then how was the number of parliamentary representatives to be fixed? If it were decided by the ratio of the population of Scotland to the population of England, the number would be over eighty. If it were decided by the proportion contributed to the joint revenue by Scotland, it would be thirteen. Not until 23 July was the Treaty completed and presented to the queen. It contained twenty-five articles, of which the most important were the first, second, third and twenty-second. The first declared that the two countries were to be united under the name of Great Britain, the second guaranteed the Hanoverian succession, the third announced that there was to be one parliament for the two kingdoms, while the twenty-second fixed the

**176**

number of Scottish representatives in the Commons at forty-five and in the Lords at sixteen. To compensate for the inevitable increase in taxation an Equivalent of £398,085 10s. was to be paid to Scotland, and exemption from various taxes, most of them temporary, was given. The Scottish law courts and system of private law were to be preserved intact, the privileges of the royal burghs and the feudal jurisdictions of the nobles were to remain inviolate. On the other hand, there was to be a common coinage and system of weights and measures, and the arms of Scotland were to be conjoined with those of England on the royal coat of arms and the national flags.

On 3 October the Scottish parliament assembled for its last session. Never again would the people of Edinburgh see the Lord Commissioner ride in state from Holyrood to the Parliament House, preceded by heralds and trumpeters, commissioners of the burghs, commissioners of the shires, lords on foot and earls on horseback. But men could give little thought to this old-world pageantry. Outside parliament only the commercial classes were in favour of the Union. The Presbyterian clergy, the inhabitants of the smaller towns and, of course, the Jacobites were all bitterly opposed to it. Within parliament all was uncertainty. Of the two hundred members only about eighty, the old Court Party, could be counted on to vote for the Treaty. The Jacobites muttered threats of rebellion, but the Jacobites were led by the Duke of Hamilton, who thundered defiance at the House one day, and next day, when vigorous action was expected from him, stayed at home because he had toothache. In the Country Party were to be found the bitterest opponents of the Union, but one section of this party, lately nicknamed 'the Squadrone Volante', maintained an obstinate silence as to its intentions.

**177**

October was spent in a general discussion of the articles. Not until 1 November was it moved that the first article be put to the vote. The motion was the signal for a furious debate that lasted for three days. At the end the motion was carried by a hundred and fifteen votes to eighty-three. The Squadrone had saved the Treaty, for the twenty-two votes that they gave were enough to turn the balance. But it looked as if much might happen before the final article was passed. Every day the Parliament House was beset by a roaring crowd. Once the Commissioner's coach and six rattled down the High Street and the Canongate pursued by an angry mob. A riot broke out in Glasgow and lasted for the better part of a month. In one town the Treaty was burned, and from every quarter of the kingdom petitions against the Union poured in. Queensberry, the Commissioner, protested that his life was in danger and that he despaired of the Treaty. A threatened Jacobite rebellion in the south failed because at the last moment Hamilton refused to act. The government acted with energy. An Act of Security passed on 12 November pledged the government to maintain the Church of Scotland as it was then established and so reassured the Presbyterian stalwarts. Troops guarded the Parliament House and lined the streets. The Commissioner never went out without an escort, and an Act was passed prohibiting unauthorized assemblies of armed men. The result of the session was now a foregone conclusion, but each article was debated with the same fire and eloquence, for each side could boast orators of the highest order, and not until 16 January 1707 did Queensberry touch the Act with the sceptre as a token that the royal assent had been granted. Another Act determined the method by which members of parliament were to be elected. The sixteen peers were to be appointed by their fellows at the begin-

**178**

ning of each parliament. Of the forty-five members of the Commons, thirty were to be appointed by freeholders in the counties having land worth more than forty shillings a year. The remaining fifteen were to be elected by the sixty-six royal burghs.

The Treaty was next submitted to the English parliament in an ingenious Bill. The preamble contained the Treaty itself, the Act of Security for safeguarding Presbyterianism in Scotland, an Act safeguarding Episcopacy in England and the Act appointing the method of electing Scottish members, while the rest of the Bill consisted of an enacting clause. The opponents of the Treaty were thus precluded from attacking the Bill in detail. It passed rapidly through both Houses, and on 6 March it received the royal assent. A fortnight later it was presented to the Scottish parliament, and on 25 March the Estates of Scotland assembled for the last time in the old Parliament Hall. What thoughts passed through the minds of the members we can only guess. No note of regret can be detected in Queensberry's formal speech of thanks. To some, like Chancellor Seafield, it was only 'the end of an auld sang'. Others, even those who had worked most strenuously for the Treaty, may have felt an irrational misgiving when they knew that no man could undo what they had done. The crown, the sceptre, the sword of state were borne out, to be lost for a hundred years. The Commissioner, the scarlet-robed peers, the lairds and burgesses filed for the last time under the tapestried walls and through the great doorway to the cowed and sullen crowds outside. Te Deums might be sung in St Paul's, the guns of the Tower might thunder the news to a rejoicing London, but many a Scotsman felt that day that his country had received a mortal wound with the loss of its status as an independent nation, let alone that of a kingdom.

**179**

# CHAPTER XIV

# POSTSCRIPT: THE JACOBITES

Eight years after the Union of the Parliaments, the Jacobites came out, encouraged by the unpopularity of the Union and the management of Scottish affairs from London. But from the beginning the rebellion lacked organized plan and timed cohesion between its various forces and lacked a leader able to give it either. The Earl of Mar raised the royal standard on 6 September 1715. A detachment that struck south to join a Border and North of England ploy suffered from too many commanders, English and Scots, and they more or less argued themselves into a surrender at Preston. That was on 14 November. On the 13th Mar had met Argyll at Sherriffmuir and fought a bloody but indecisive battle that he allowed, in the succeeding weeks, to become his defeat.

It was to this situation that Prince James Francis Edward Stewart, the son of James VIII, came when he arrived at last in Peterhead about Christmas. He was not the inspiring personality his son was to be, and the difficult job of putting fresh life into downcast troops was beyond him. Early in February James had sailed again for France, Mar with him, and there was left behind the memory of a somewhat melancholy Stewart but little else to offset the inevitable reprisals – headings, hangings and forfeitures.

Perhaps the most significant thing in the thirty years between the two risings was the birth of a son to Prince James and Clementina Sobieski in 1720. The Highlanders had their future leader, and one of a very different spirit from his father. But there was no thought of the '45 at that time. So long as Jacobite clans could raise a second rent for exiled chiefs the Stewart cause still had friends in the north. There was seen to be coming, too, a time when the cause might need its friends again, for Britain was at war once more in Europe and France was thinking of counter-invasion with Jacobite backing. The decisive argument for seizing an opportunity was not an argument at all but a man – the Young Chevalier.

Charles Edward Stewart was in his twenty-third year at this point and a prince of gallant grace. He was a Stewart of the old house in looks, vigour and charm. He brought a touch of Sobieski fire to the old Stewart courage and wore both with a laughing gallantry that was never more evident than in the face of heavy odds or danger. He lacked perhaps the best of his ancestors' intelligence, but he was far from being a fool. His greatest asset for the immediate task in hand was an instant grasp of Highland temper, an instinctive understanding of that complex make-up that gave him a basis for clan leadership as firm and profound as Montrose's had been. What was missing was Montrose's training in arms.

Even so his quality had gone north before him, and the manner of his arrival gave proof of it. Early in 1744 there had been 10,000 French troops, with a military genius in command, waiting at Dunkirk for the moment of invasion. A year later it was gone on other business. France was less urgent in the affair despite victorious possession of Flanders, and although Charles chose a good moment he sailed with only two ships, the larger of which met a British man-o'-war and had to return, taking most of his supplies with it. Charles went on, with the famous Seven Men of Moidart and little

**181**

more except his own gallant hope, and on 23 May 1745 reached Eriskay, an island in Barra Sound. Two days later he had crossed the Minch and landed at Loch nan Uamh, to the dismay of the chiefs and the eager anticipation of the clans. By the end of August, a fortnight or so after the raising of the standard at Glenfinnan, Charles had some 2,000 men with him, MacDonalds mostly, under Clanranald, Glengarry and Keppoch, with Stewart of Ardshiel, but also Camerons under the young Lochiel. The rising of the '45 was under way.

The odds were long, but not so long as to make Charles's venture 'the senseless prank of an unschooled boy', as a Whig historian has called it. It is true that the chiefs had not expected his arrival – the last move of Jacobite planning in Scotland that year had been one of dissuasion in view of the uncertainty of French support. Moreover, the cause in Scotland was far from winning national support even on paper.

Charles went on. There had been swift initial encouragement; a detachment of Government troops marching from Fort Augustus to Fort William had fallen to the MacDonalds in an encounter more of strategy than of arms, and the clansmen were jubilant. General Cope, in command of the regulars in Scotland, moved north from Stirling in the expectation that Charles would make for Inverness, but the Prince outflanked him and descended on Perth, and while Cope was sailing back from Aberdeen to defend Edinburgh, Charles was entering the capital. Three days later Cope landed at Dunbar, and in no very good fettle approached an enemy who had already out-generalled him. The clans fell on him at Prestonpans on 21 September, and in a matter of minutes Cope was in flying retreat to Berwick.

Charles was strong for the march south, but there was division when he held council. It has been said that the clans disliked the idea of invading England – a ploy that held no happy memories for them. But there was also the question of strategy, to be a matter of difference between Charles and his lieutenants. The prince was all for the bold course, and there was much to be said for the shock of boldness, the success of which was certain to expedite French aid. But his commanders, notably Lord George Murray, were less certain, for there had been no sign of any sympathetic rising across the Border, there was a strong force under General Wade at Newcastle, and if French aid really were coming it might be more readily sent to Scottish than to English soil.

There was success at the end of the march, too, for Wade was imprisoned in Newcastle by November weather that blocked the roads for transport, and Charles made himself master of Carlisle with little difficulty. But the dissension in command that was to be the ruin of the whole enterprise had already shown itself once and was to do so increasingly. After Carlisle there was division about the next move, which finally resolved itself into a march on Manchester, reached on 29 November. Government forces were positioned strategically ahead and on the flanks of the Jacobite army – the Duke of Cumberland was up now. Murray and his officers were for turning back, but Charles and the more daring spirits were for pressing on. It was decided to go as far as Derby in the hope of news of the French or of brisker recruiting, and Derby was reached. There Charles's commanders bluntly refused to go farther.

The retreat was pursued by Wade and Cumberland, but it was not a flight, for when Cumberland's advance guard caught up with the rear of the retreat near Penrith there was a sharp little action that ended any but cautious pursuit. The true feeling of the country, however, was made plain now. What

**183**

had been at best disguised English indifference on the march south was open hostility on the way north. It was clear that any future for the rising lay in Scotland. Meanwhile the retreating army had crossed the Border, levied a fine on hostile Dumfries and by the end of the year was in Glasgow, resting and replenishing with some sorely needed supplies – which the city was exceedingly reluctant to furnish. The two months that had now passed had seen some activity in Scotland. Duncan Forbes of Culloden, acting for the government, had succeeded in neutralizing the Whig clans of the far north and in raising troops to reinforce the available regulars. But he had not succeeded with the wily Simon Lovat, who held back himself but let his Frasers go out under his 'undutiful son'. There was also a rally of MacKenzies to the prince's standard, an access of strength in guns and professional soldiers under Perth's brother, and a Gordon grip on Aberdeen and the northeast. Altogether Charles could count on some 8,000 men against forces in Scotland much smaller – and this Jacobite strength invited action.

It came, at Stirling. Charles had marched on and easily taken the town, but the castle held out, and there now moved up to its relief a strong government force under General Hawley, who had superseded Cope. He had no better luck than his predecessor, however, for at Falkirk he was outmanoeuvred and routed, his dragoons disorganized by the clansmen's apparent imperviousness to a mounted charge. But the victory was short-lived. Charles wanted to stay and secure Stirling. Cumberland had rallied Hawley's fugitives and was coming up at last; and the clansmen were not of the mettle to relish the slow siege of a stronghold like Stirling Castle. But to eager spirits the thing had the look of another Derby, so that on the morrow of victory came what amounted to moral defeat.

**184**

Charles marched to meet Cumberland, and as the two armies approached he ventured, against advice (but not, for once, against Murray's advice), a night march as prelude to a surprise attack. The manoeuvre failed through misjudgment of terrain and marching capacity. There was a retreat without attack, and it was finally a fatigued and sleep-weary force that Cumberland encountered at Drumossie Moor, near Culloden. Lord George Murray disliked the ground chosen and with reason, for it gave ample opportunity for the play of Cumberland's guns and dragoons while offering little advantage for the Highlanders' pet tactics of downward charge behind targe and claymore. Legend attributes the disaster that followed to the hurt pride of the MacDonalds, denied the position of honour on the right of the line. The clansmen's defeat was simply the defeat of a small and poorly equipped force by a larger and better armed one. Cumberland's guns did deadly work, and when the Highland charge that they provoked broke his first line, his second line was ready to crumple it up as it swept through. And that was the end of the '45 – but for two things.

One was the era of savagely vindictive punishment that followed Culloden. The fear of a badly frightened government turned to a fury of hate. Cumberland was given a free hand and more than earned his new title of 'Butcher'. The other was the romance of the prince's wanderings in the west and final escape. There was a £30,000 reward for his capture – no one betrayed him. Troops swept the Highlands in search of him, burning, killing, torturing – all in vain. Charles was with his own people, and they hid him, through a thousand escapes and alarms that make a Jacobite Odyssey, reaching a climax at last in the wit and courage of Flora MacDonald's exploit of getting him safely away to France.

**185**

# APPENDIX

# 𝑅ULERS OF THE KINGDOM
# OF SCOTLAND

| | | | |
|---|---|---|---|
| Kenneth I | c.843–58 | William I | 1165–1214 |
| Donald I | 858–62 | Alexander II | 1214–49 |
| Constantine I | 862–77 | Alexander III | 1249–86 |
| Aed | 877–8 | Margaret | 1286–90 |
| Giric/Eochaid | 878–89 | Interregnum | 1290–92 |
| Donald II | 889–900 | John | 1292–96 |
| Constantine II | 900–943 | Interregnum | 1296–1306 |
| Malcolm I | 943–54 | Robert I | 1306–29 |
| Indulf | 954–62 | David II | 1329–71 |
| Dubh | 962-66 | Robert II | 1371–90 |
| Culen | 966–71 | Robert III | 1390–1406 |
| Kenneth II | 971–95 | James I | 1406–37 |
| Constantine III | 995–97 | James II | 1437–60 |
| Kenneth III/Giric | 997?–1005 | James III | 1460–88 |
| Malcolm II | 1005–34 | James IV | 1488–1513 |
| Duncan I | 1034–40 | James V | 1513–42 |
| Macbeth | 1040–57 | Mary I | 1542–67 |
| Lulach | 1057–58 | James VI | 1567–1625 |
| Malcolm III | 1058–93 | Charles I | 1625–49 |
| Donald III | 1093–94 | Charles II | 1649–85 |
| Duncan II | 1094 | (in exile 1651–60) | |
| Donald III | 1094–97 | James VII | 1685–89 |
| Edgar | 1097–1107 | William II ⎤ | 1689–1702 |
| Alexander I | 1107–24 | Mary II  ⎦ | 1689–94 |
| David I | 1124–53 | Anne | 1702–1707 |
| Malcolm IV | 1153–65 | | |